# THE NEW MODEL OF **TERTIARY EDUCATIONAL INSTITUTION** IN **POSTWAR SIERRA LEONE**

Dr. Michael Nicolas Wundah

authorHOUSE®

*AuthorHouse™ UK*
*1663 Liberty Drive*
*Bloomington, IN 47403 USA*
*www.authorhouse.co.uk*
*Phone: 0800.197.4150*

*Published by AuthorHouse 04/01/2016*

*ISBN: 978-1-5246-3152-9 (sc)*
*ISBN: 978-1-5246-3153-6 (hc)*
*ISBN: 978-1-5246-3154-3 (e)*

*Print information available on the last page.*

# Contents

## Part Nine

## Part Ten

## Part Eleven

# Dedication

This book is dedicated to all patriotic and progressive Sierra Leoneans, living at home and abroad. All those who choose IAMTECH over other tertiary institutions in Sierra Leone deserve this book. Their courage and sensible decision to make this choice has inspired the writing of this book among other things. IAMTECH assures all candidates that its doors are always open to those who seek solace in its philosophy and motto: "For Country and For Humanity"

Finally, I dedicate this book to the relentless contributions of Professor Dr Paul Kamara and his dedicated wife, Dr Mrs Abie Paula Kamara. Their decision to invest in an educational project that shall be a lasting legacy of the values of patriotism and constructive nationalism will never be forgotten.

# Acknowledgements

I can't afford to acknowledge all those that have contributed in diverse ways to the writing of this book. IAMTECH is a large family so should any attempt be made to do so, we will end up with endless tributes. All the same I must acknowledge some individuals. First and foremost, I am grateful to my family, my beautiful and supportive wife, Mrs Aji Ansu Sarr-Wundah, my two lovely sons Mr Ebrima Tamba Wundah and Master Wahkar Nyuma Wundah and their siblings in Sierra Leone. They are my muses, the pillars of my strength.

I must say a big thank you to them for the enormous sacrifices we have made together. Together we have decided that I return home and serve our motherland. May Allah, the Good Lord, continually enrich their blessings!

To the IAMTECH family, firmly, united in ideas as we affectionately refer to ourselves as a closely knit institution. I would like to express my special thanks and gratitude to everyone of this great union.

The proprietors and co-founders- Professor Dr Paul Kamara and his wife, Dr Mrs Abie Paula Kamara are awesome. They truly deserve this book. Husband and wife shall go down in the history of education in Sierra Leone for their enormous contributions to the first private tertiary institution that has made a huge mark on the sector.

The principal, Dr Mrs Lauretta Will-Sillah; Professor Patrick FU Taylor, Vice Principal Academic Affairs; Dr Obai Fullah- Director Distance Learning and Dean of Students; Alhaji Mohamed Salieu Kamara the Registrar, Alhaji Bakar, Deputy Registrar, Mr Stephen Lamin Examinations Officer and his assistant Mr Kabia, all the deans, heads of departments and all the lecturers, especially Mr Sulayman Koroma, Mr Turay, Mr Sankoh, Mr Ibrahim John Bangura, Mr Cummings, the two Mrs Massaquois at the Brookfields Learning Centere, the intelligent and bookworm, Mr Thomas at the Circular Road Learning Centere, the special assistant to the CEO Mr Andrew Tarawalli alias "Uncle T". He is quite an articulate and talented guy. The innovative and dedicated Miss Maseray Mansaray and her boss, Mrs Songu at the Kono Learning Centere, and those at Lunsar, Rokupr, Kambia and Bo Learning Centeres are all awesome people.

The college librarian, his assistant and members of the College Canteen, the newly elected Student Union Executive are worth recognizing. Not forgetting the fact that historic milestone has been reached at IAMTECH. For the first time in the history of IAMTECH and perhaps the tertiary sector in Sierra Leone, the students have elected the first female student union President. Her name is Miss Aminata Turay. I wish her government, especially Thomas, a member of her cabinet, good luck in their endeavours.

The educative and informative inputs of all those I have mentioned and the ones I couldn't due to space constraints have been vital for the writing of this book. I have utilized their inputs in order to underscore the salient points which form the cornerstones of the aims, objectives and philosophy of IAMTECH.

My acknowledgements will be incomplete if I fail to pay tribute to the Ministry of Education Science and Technology (MEST). I have utilized some of the papers which were presented during the Week of Education 2015, symposium at the Miata Conference Centre from 7 to 12 December 2015.

My good friends at the finance office are special, ambitious young men and a lady. Their boss the young, clever, unassuming Mr Peter Umaru Kamara answered some of my questions about the history of the college. Congratulations to him, he wedded recently to the beauty of his life, affectionately known as Kadija.

This young man portrays a breath of fresh air. No sooner had I switched on my laptop on New Year's Day in order to do the final editing of this book in my London parlour, than I received a call from him to wish me and my family a Happy New Year. His able assistant finance officer is the soft-spoken, clever, and ever smiling Mr Bakar.

The auditor of the college, Mrs Matilda Wright is very friendly but officious in all that she does. She is clever with numbers too, a job she has done all her life. Now and again this lady and her colleagues put sweet smiles on my face when my ideas are temporary in retreat.

The entire staff in the office of the principal including Miss Beatrice and Mrs Kamara were supportive. Maseray and her hardworking staff at the business centre, Mrs Abdulai the procurement officer, Mr M.K the estate officer, the entire staff in the registry, the quiet computer genius, Mr Bangura (Professor Taylor's Special Aide, who is also one of our senior lecturers), Alhaji, the College Health Officer and Mr Foday, the senior driver and one of his junior drivers, Mr Mohammed, are well noted for their contributions in many ways.

Mr Mohammed is the Master of Cutting Corners in the history of driving. By cutting corners, he often made our ways around the busy streets of Freetown easily. Painstakingly, this young man drove me around Freetown in the absence of his real boss the principal.

I want to thank our smart and dutiful security officers. Making a crucial contribution, the catering team in the College Canteen have fed me with the most delicious dishes. They have energized and kept me going ever since I arrived at IAMTECH. Muda at the SLRA subsidized my food too. She is an excellent caterer. The technicians, mechanics, builders, messengers and cleaners are very entertaining. Their jokes raised my spirits.

I am inspired by a student nicknamed "IT" by his college mates. He is one of our most ambitious and dedicated students at IAMTECH. Coming from a humble background, and now reading for a degree course at IAMTECH, makes him my type of notable student who inspires others. He is also very helpful and obedient. He diligently, serves Professor Taylor and the principal, Dr Mrs Lauretta Will-Sillah. I must confess that his level of inspiration touched me when I suffered intermittent writer's block.

My acknowledgements will be incomplete unless I recognize the unfailing contributions of one particular institution in Sierra Leone. I want to thank Professor Kosonike Koso-Thomas chairman, his executive secretary Professor David Koroma and their colleagues at the Tertiary Education Commission (TEC). They have recast the mechanism of tertiary education in the country. I wish them well in their endeavours.

I must admit that there are awesome people at this college. Such is the degree of care and love they have showered on me since I joined them. Each time I felt the burden of writing I sought solace in their mature, understanding, bountiful smiles and welcoming attitudes. How awesome! I pray they become ever aware that this book belongs to all of us at IAMTECH and our families at home and abroad. It belongs to Sierra Leone, the country we all dearly love.

Above all I owe it to my Creator, the Living God for giving me the strength and wisdom to write this book.

# Preface

When I finally decided to work for IAMTECH in April 2015, I knew that the moment had come for me to start and finish this book project. I'd realized then that a comprehensive story of the unique contributions the founders of this college have made to education in Sierra Leone are worth recording for all to read and learn from as productive and inspiring strategies.

Prior to the commencement of the project, Dr Mrs Abie Paula Kamara had played the role of the co-master of ceremonies (MC) when we launched the biography of Dr Christiana Thorpe which I authored two years ago. Professor Dr Paul Kamara also attended the ceremony. Dr Mrs Kamara is a teacher by profession. She fancies, admires and enjoys artistic, literary accomplishments.

On that occasion, there was an immense outpouring of the finest and richest of tributes in honour of Dr Thorpe. The First Lady, Her Excellency Mrs Sia Nyama Koroma was the chief launcher of the book. Her tributes were sustained by other distinguished dignitaries who graced the occasion.

It was on that historic occasion that my instincts were confirmed. It was pivotal to the outcomes that inspired the writing of this book. IAMTECH is dear to the hearts of the founders as well as all those associated with the college. Over the years it has touched many souls within Sierra Leone and beyond.

This book discusses some of the main differences between the model of tertiary education that IAMTECH offers to her clients and those followed by other tertiary institutions in the country. The IAMTECH model hinges on the ideal type of education that post war Sierra Leone requires in order to inspire the restoration and maximization of national economic growth and development.

The ideal type is informed by liberal values and promotes the human face that should be put to the policies and management of education. The book narrates at length the values and culture which the IAMTECH ideal type typifies. The college recognizes the critical, nexus between education and the requirements, challenges and opportunities prevalent in modern job markets. This nexus has become more profound in the twenty-first century than ever before.

However with the Lord on their side they were elevated to the spotlight, which they took advantage of through hard work and faith in their Creator. They have imbibed their philosophy.

They relish a profound philosophy that reflects the motto of the institute. It is "For Country and For Humanity", meaning, that education becomes worthwhile and fulfils its promises when it serves the interests of country and humanity. In short, education should be a public good not merely for the few privileged, powerful elites. Diversification serves as one of the core values of the institute's motto and by extension its philosophy.

IAMTECH is set to celebrate its silver jubilee in the early months of 2016. On behalf of my family at home and abroad, I congratulate this great institution and its founders and staff and wish them more successes! Now that the endeavours of Paul and Paula have gained fruits, their relentless efforts deserve a written record as part and parcel of their legacy. It is gratifying to note that things are going splendidly at IAMTECH.

Happy and prosperous 2016 and congratulations to the founders and the entire workforce!

MNW 12January 2016

# PART ONE

# 1

# Rationale

This book tells an amazing story and bears an exciting title. It is *The New Model of Tertiary Education in Post-War Sierra Leone*. It is a new project in the real sense of the word due to what it means and stands for. The rationale that informs the project defines tertiary education differently. The functions and impacts tertiary education has on society at large justify its definition. This new model of tertiary education has impacted tremendously on the people of Sierra Leone in many ways. That is why it is unique.

Its narratives are centered on the handiwork, philosophy and ideals of one Sierra Leonean couple. They are the architects of the new model of tertiary education under discussion. Their admirers affectionately call them Paul and Paula. Brilliantly, they have crafted this new model of higher education in the private sector at a time when many questions have been asked about the functions, outcomes and overall impact of higher education in Sierra Leone. Their new model is distinct in many ways from those offered by sister tertiary institutions in the country.

The institution that professes the new model is on the lips of everyone in the country. It is called the Institute of Advanced Management and Technology (IAMTECH). It is renowned for the relevant skills and qualifications it offers and the values it stands for. IAMTECH offers the ideal type of education. It matches the challenges and fulfils the promises of the ideal type of tertiary education fit for the twenty-first century.

It means that at such a time like this, tertiary education could only be deemed the ideal type if it prepares students for the challenges and opportunities of the twenty-first century and beyond. In addition to its values the college has also redefined the meaning and functions of twenty-first century tertiary education and taken it to a new and different place.

That new place symbolizes the new landscape that underpins the key values of IAMTECH. In fact one could argue that it has not only redefined the functions and essence of tertiary education in Sierra Leone. It has profoundly impacted practically on lives and the political and socioeconomic development of the country.

The institution holds that the ideal type of tertiary education is holistic only if it serves the purpose and interests of the nation. IAMTECH has substantially withstood these tests to the admiration of society at large. The adage goes that hard work backed by efficiency pays. IAMTECH is about hard work and the unwavering determination to succeed and to share that success with country and humanity.

---

It is through this philosophy and belief that IAMTECH has made tremendous gains and brought into the tertiary sector a new realization. At the heart of the new realization which is on the lips of everyone, is the enviable word or unique concept *quality*. That prompts the question. What is the new realization about? The new realization is that there is a cogent relationship, a nexus between quality education and the chances of inspiring and maximizing the socioeconomic prosperity of a nation.

By extension, quality education enhances social cohesion and political stability. How? Quality education provides job opportunities. More often than not, it is those who acquire the quality skills and qualifications who stand the chances of securing the lucrative, well paid jobs and these real assets such jobs bring.

More often than not, quality education brings comfort and peace into the homes and lives of people. Research evidence does suggest that when for example young people are in gainful employment, they are more likely to be kept off the streets. This reality is evident in most Third World countries where unemployment among youths has been tied to lack of relevant skills and qualifications.

IAMTECH has a meaningful motto which crowns the philosophy, values and ideals of the proprietors and founders. That motto is "For Country and For Humanity" Since its inception, it is gratifying to note that the institution has translated the values and ideals of this motto into its teaching and learning outcomes and the employment statistics of the institution. That the college has earned tremendous successes today is due to the fact that this motto is the key component of what it takes to offer what is defined as quality and ideal type of education in modernity.

Moreover, it has translated the values of this motto and its underlying philosophy into the relationship between educational pursuits and service to country and humanity. All of these values have impacted positively on students, local communities and the country at large.

Factor the values of the motto of the college and its philosophy into the wider ramifications associated with the acquisition of quality education. It underscores the fact that education that serves the interests of country and humanity is the ideal type and that the ideal type of education serves the public good. To reiterate once more, this new model emphasizes that skills and qualifications only make sense these days if they have tangible meaning in people's lives. This reality does not in any way diminish the intrinsic values that we acquire from education.

When education helps nations to attain progress and development, undoubtedly it makes real meaning in the lives of the citizenry and their country that is dear to their hearts. Education should be provided for everyone, especially the disadvantaged. It should provide those who successfully achieve the necessary skills and qualification with good jobs and other related opportunities, so that they can be useful citizens to themselves and society.

---

Educationalists are united on the idea that liberalism is at the heart of the ideal type of education. The exponents as well as those who achieve the ideal type of education practice liberal values. In a liberal society the opportunities that come with education constitute basic fundamental human rights. It means that education is not a privilege but everyone's right.

Hence no one should be denied the right to a decent education. That should be the case because education as a public good puts those who pursue it in good stead to fulfil their civic responsibilities. They will be well placed to enjoy their fundamental, constitutional rights as long as they obey the provisions of the constitution.

Based on an analysis of the liberal values of education and what it offers, there is no doubt that the benefits go beyond a selected few or a privileged class of communities. In other words the opportunities that education provides should not be meant only for the selected few in society.

On the contrary, in some less developed countries, educational opportunities, especially at the higher tier, are made available only for the privileged, rich and powerful few. In such countries meritocracy has been subsumed to elitist policies and ideology. Hence the values of egalitarianism are severely hampered. These are the vices that the new model of tertiary education espoused and practiced by IAMTECH and her proprietors is determined to relegate to the abyss.

# 2

# Liberals

"When I first met Paul and Paula little did I know that they are liberals to the core. With the passage of time, my misgivings about them changed. They are the most liberal type I have ever met in my life"

The above allusions constitute the candid opinions of one of the neighbours of the family. They lived in the United Kingdom as neighbours for years. Amazingly the speaker is also a relative of theirs.

Here are other opinions about Paul and Paula on the subject of liberalism as the lynchpin which also underpins the beliefs and philosophy of the couple.

"Liberals or liberalism is a tricky political jargon these days. While some may describe liberals or liberal-minded personalities as kind-hearted, fair and just, others may hold a different view altogether"

I smiled as I asked "What is the contrary view or views?"

"The contrary view may be that liberals are political rattlesnakes who splash kindness or they are similar to desperate politicians that dish out doles for publicity stunts, whilst they have hidden agendas or motives"

"So which of the two views would you attribute to Paula and Paul?"I pressed him further.

"I will subscribe the first attribute to Paula and her husband of course!"

"Why?" I asked.

"They both have hearts of gold. The Lord shall surely continue to multiply their blessings"

The third contributor made these comments passionately about the couple: "Paula and I were schoolmates I know she does not recognize that we were not only schoolmates but we lived in the same neighbourhood in Kissy as teenagers. She lived with her aunt at that time. She is not only kind, she is the type that cries with others in need, and helps them as the need arises"

Undoubtedly, Paul and Paula are true liberals in their attitudes, perceptions and values. They have ensured that their educational project practices these values by impacting on communities and society.

---

One has to argue that the couples were influenced by English values. They spent decades in England and acquired their qualifications there as well, so they surely emulated the English culture, at the heart of which are liberal values.

Liberal values hold that education should not be for the powerful, wealthy few. It is not for those connected to the ruling or wealthy elite. It is for all and sundry, which makes it a public good. Long before they dreamed of this project they had long dreaded the bottleneck problem that Sierra Leone's higher education suffered.

From the 1970s to the early 1990s, most students hadn't the opportunity to enter the mainstream universities due to this persistent bottleneck culture. Paul and Paula were obviously determined to minimize, if not, eradicate completely, this bottleneck predicament in post-war Sierra Leone.

Another key characteristic for which they are known is their faith in one philosophy. They believe that education should have a national as well as humanist bent. In this context they profoundly believe in the philosophy that an educated person should be of tremendous service to his or her country and humanity. By the time they founded IAMTECH, they had thought of how the type of education that radiates their beliefs that define their philosophy should equally radiate in the lives of fellow Sierra Leoneans. Cleverly and proactively, Paul and Paula have ensured that this philosophy is conveyed by the eye-catching motto of IAMTECH.

The amazing philosophy of IAMTECH is broad and has been theoretically and practically articulated in the course contents of its programmes since its inception as a tertiary institution. These are some of the positive and functional impacts the college has made on tertiary education.

---

i. It has made an impressive and productive mark on the lives of its graduates by making their skills and qualifications easily marketable.

ii. As a result of its contributions to national development, it is recognized as a lasting national treasure and legacy.

iii. It is recognized as the ideal typical of tertiary institution similar to the ones found in developed countries.

iv. It cherishes inclusiveness and diversification in education.

v. It has made education accessible to the inaccessible communities of the country. Through its distance learning programmes it has reached many people across the length and breadth of the nation.

vi. Above all, the proprietors and founders are proud to acknowledge the country they richly serve, Sierra Leone, as their homeland. That is why they chose to establish this new model of tertiary education that serves the social, economic and political needs of the country.

---

The success stories of the institutions hinge on quality assurance. In the past decades quality assurance as the needed commodity has been in short supply, especially at the tertiary level. The college has cemented its distinct characteristics by ensuring quality assurance is preserved at all cost. It incumbent on lecturers as well as teachers to ensure they play strictly by the rules regarding assessments, behaviours and conduct.

Below are the enlightening comments made by one of the experts of their overseas quality stocktaking associates and organisations. IAMTECH has had a professional, academic relationship with them, close to four years.

The comments are reproduced in the original form. I had an exclusive tête-à-tête with him.

I started by telling the expert to reveal to me his candid opinion about the general, quality procedures and status of the college verbally. I must state that the comments were very frank and forthright.

"Reflecting on the quality assurance files kept by your institution, we must commend you for your steadfastness and quality education you provide at IAMTECH. The last time our leading experts visited you in Sierra Leone in order to update our quality assurance portfolios, they noted that you were far ahead of the other providers in most institution in the Sub-Sahara region"

I have to warn that this was in no way trying to be interrogatory. We were only having a sincere conversation. However we both knew that I was writing this book and the expert knows my official relationship with IAMTECH. The questions and entire conversation was conducted in good faith.

So I asked the expert further to scribble some detailed comments on the same subject matter. I must confess that I was amazed by what the expert came up with:

The title read *Wholesale Quality Summary*:

i.   The institution has comprehensive, up-to-date quality assurance files.

ii.  The contents of the files clearly spell out the criteria/guidelines for the quality assurance performances as stipulated by our organization and national standards.

iii. Students' portfolios contents are up-to-date.

iv.  Their work products are both theoretical and practical and they are in line with our quality assurance prescriptions and standards and the national guidelines.

v.   The programmes and qualifications you offer are authentic and of high standards.

vi.  You make your provisions available to quality assurance inspections and audits as stipulated by us.

vii. The institution has qualified and professionally experienced lecturers capable of delivering the programmes to good effect.

viii. Your criteria for admission of students into the programmes are authentic and in line with your country's as well as our organization's standards.

The conclusion was even more exciting and thrilling to imagine. It was the icing on the cake. "We are quite impressed. Please keep it up!"

Let us return to part of the title of the book. The phrase or key word *"new model"* in the title is extremely inspiring and has biblical connotations too. This makes it as tempting as provocative for most analysts because it appeals as well as raises all sorts of questions. It creates all sorts of permutations in the minds of critical thinkers. It is also as amazing as debatable such that any theorist and practical analyst would sink his or her teeth into it.

Above all, when applied to how Sierra Leone's tertiary sector has affected society at large, the connotations of the phrase or adage become even more suggestive. From a generic point of view, the title inspires meaningful food for thought.

For example take the challenges and opportunities education offers and fails to offer. Some may argue that the failings of education are due to unforeseeable circumstances. Others may differ and argue instead to the contrary that the onus of making education works and pays dividends for people is incumbent on the manner in which man himself or people react to the opportunities and challenges education presents. It means that those made of sterner stuff, more often than not, seize their opportunities, face their challenges squarely, and maximize the benefits of the outcomes of education.

Some are weak, to the extent that they are prone to fail easily in the pursuits of their dreams in life. These pursuits or dreams could be associated with education, politics or business, trade or commerce. Literally speaking, some argue that those who usually succeed are determined and hard-working. In brief, they are personalities that are made of steel. Made of steel means they are strong, and compact enough to endure and surmount all kinds of problems in order to achieve their goals.

To sum up the analogies and arguments, I have given examples of two different potential or imagined candidates or aspirants for educational and other related pursuits or endeavours. In terms of educational pursuits the first category includes those who can pursue and successfully complete their studies no matter the obstacles they encounter. By contrast, the second category comprises those who fail or drop out of educational institution, simply because they can't cope with the challenges they may encounter.

The latter candidates or aspirants are referred to by critics as the weaker vessels of humankind. The new model of education offered by IAMTECH is well equipped materially and professionally to deal with the problems of the second category the would-be, failed aspirants or contestants in the race to pursue education or politics or business enterprises.

The professionally trained and qualified lecturers at IAMTECH are competent to deal with the complex situations and conditions that prevail in modern-day classrooms. They are capable of dealing with all sorts of students from different socioeconomic and political backgrounds. This is because they are aware of the fact that learners differ considerably in terms of their learning styles.

It is incumbent on teachers or lecturers to recognize the varying learning styles and degrees of competences of learners, along with their varying backgrounds and deal with them successfully. It is no secret that the history of Sierra Leone, especially the socioeconomic as well as the psychological impact of the civil war grossly affects some people's ability to learn.

The competent and professionally trained tutors, instructors at IAMETCH are aware of these realities. There is abundant evidence that they are capable of reconciling the inherent differences there are in mixed ability classes in modern day classroom practice, in particular the differences which characterize post-war Sierra Leone.

In fact lecturers have maximized the positive learning outcomes identified and properly utilized them in mixed ability groups for the benefits of the entire class. Most significantly, the massive rates of students that have gone through the institution successfully as well as gained lucrative jobs in the system confirm my claims.

It should not also go unnoticed that the college was founded during the warring years in Sierra Leone. Hence, these professionals are not new to the wider ramifications of that brutal civil war.

In terms of which appropriate methodology and resources they should apply to successfully deal with problematic students, they are definitely on top of their game. In addition, they are very much aware of the saying which states that the weakest link should not be allowed to derail the escalating strengths and capabilities of the determined and energized train, be it locomotive or electrical engine.

# 3

# Inner Thoughts

The new model of tertiary education in post war Sierra Leone espouses an expansive philosophy with considerable inner thoughts that defeats narrow mindedness, selfishness and fickle mindedness. In addition to the fact that education is transient, the inner thoughts of the policymakers should be influenced by the wider context in which failings of education have dampened the nation's general spirit.

In hindsight Sierra Leone is a nation that was perceived as the gold standard in the region if not the entire continent of Africa. Reflecting on the key issues which are perceived to have impeded the system, such as the bottleneck culture and narrowness of role education plays, the inner logic and sanity of the inner thoughts must prevail.

These inner thoughts pinpoint the argument that any ideal type of education has to be transient. The inner thoughts state that education is transient and that is the reason why it is worth fighting for, tooth and nail. The fight is a worthy course and therefore, it should be fought to the finish. The second key of argument which the inner thoughts present is that the endeavours of the glorious decades were impeded by an unfinished business. Therefore, it is ideal to note that whatever agendas are set to revive and rejuvenate education in post war Sierra Leone, policymakers must ensure that one thing is done make education an essential tool of progress through the transient strategy.

The transient strategy is needed in order to acquire, and utilize the outcomes, gains, and winnings of education. It is needed so as to make the by-products of education profitable for all communities. And above these outcomes, the transient strategy is symbolized by practical skills and qualifications which are transferable in various arenas and emerge triumphant.

The Week of Education 2015 did emphasize these points as the cornerstone of the government's policy initiatives. In its recent history, Sierra Leone has faced enormous challenges. Some are of national proportion which inspired the global community to come and render their financial and moral support. It is true that no man is an island besides we live in a globalised world that has become ever smaller and reduced to a global village.

However, nation states should be self-sufficient enough in order to make meaningful contributions to the global village. The acquisition of knowledge does not only mean obtaining qualifications and relevant skills. The gains made out of education must be cogent enough to ensure nation states prestige and integrity. Sierra Leoneans welcomed and manifested gratitude to the international community for their help during the Ebola epidemic and flooding devastations.

At the same time Sierra Leoneans did ask themselves many questions: Where are our educated and learned people? Where are our nurses and doctors? What role did they play on their own and how capable were they to play tangible roles without the aid of foreign interventions? These salient questions bring us back to the necessity to ensure that our educational institutions teach transferable skills which have multidimensional functions that may be utilized at critical times.

Reflecting on the two recent national calamities, the frailties inherent in the education or skills acquisition sector were exposed. Above all they brought the widespread realization that lessons need to be learned. By implication the decline in the standards of education inspired a sense of national awareness.

For instance, the Week of Education 2015 set up a committee to review the status of the sector, determine the degree of decline and think of measures to address the problems. The findings covered all layers of the education system in Sierra Leone. The findings did not only concentrate on the tertiary sector, which is the theme of this book. Yes, IAMTECH belongs to the tertiary sector, so the findings of the Education Planning Review covered all institutions, including colleges and universities.

The committee picked up on a stark reality in their comprehensive Education Planning Review findings

"The education sector in Sierra Leone is at a cross-road. Progress from post-conflict stagnation to normal development was derailed by the Ebola crisis. But robust response to the crisis by the Ministry of Education Science and Technology (MEST), and partners has vitalized the sector. It now seems poised for response for transformation, if action is taken before the paradoxical gains from the Ebola crisis dissipate"

The above comments represent an eloquent view of the problems the sector has faced and continues to face. However one of the Review's main points is that the international community or partners may render financial and logistic aid each time Sierra Leone is embroiled in massive national problems, but that does not diminish one salient fact.

The future of the sector, like the entire fate of the state is in the hands of Sierra Leoneans. As the saying goes, they are all in this together. The solutions to the problems highlighted by the committee of reviewers rest with the polity, family and the educational institutions.

In fact it seems clear that the reviewers clamoured for the adoption of the ideal type of education whose values are the theme of this book. The ideal type of education which the new model would like to see serving the entire country has the potential to pay heed to the observations and recommendations of the committee of reviewers.

I have to continuously hammer home the point that education is transient. That is the functionally educated person should be well placed to make his skills transferable. It is at the heart of the philosophy of the new model that IAMTECH is practicing, among other things.

Education should not be idealistic it should be realistic. It underpins practical, realistic, doable and achievable values. We should not misconstrue this philosophy by thinking that it pays little or no meaning to the acquisition of theoretical knowledge. What it says is simply that theories should be backed by practical skills and knowledge of the sort that makes the pursuits of education realistic and beneficial in the short as well as the long term.

There is a related point worth mentioning. The interpretation of this philosophy is not deceptive. It is not an attempt to brainwash readers that educational pursuits is as easy as drinking water. It is not an easy walk in the park, it requires immense sacrifice. One needs to burn candles at both ends and break endless sweats in the process. Carrying out this educational philosophy entails an endless sacrifice, determination and hard work. It is about expending sweat and blood.

The second clause of this philosophy is simple but effective for the pursuits of national progress. It upholds that education or any endeavour in life poses challenges which are sometimes capable of putting the weak, feeble and vulnerable at serious risk. That is why some people are afraid to take chances or risks in life. They perceive such attempts as indulging in gambling, a game of chance.

Relate this philosophy to the observation of the reviewers of the Education Planning Review. It means that all the stakeholders of education within and outside the country need to brace themselves at this crossroads. They should choose the obvious gather themselves more than ever before and inject proactive policies in the sector, raise standards and reactivate accelerated economic diversification and growth. Failing to take these paths means that doing nothing as an option shall lead to total collapse of standards, accountability, transparency and discipline in the system.

Here is another cogent lesson from which the new Sierra Leone should learn. There is this angle that exposes a general perspective. That is to say, success or failures in life, whether in educational pursuits or related ones, depends by and large on the mental toughness and psychological makeup of individuals and their mindsets.

Let us reflect on the opinions of some of the people who attended the Week of Education 2015. Some of their positions are premised on the philosophy I have stated above.

During my interviews on the subject, my first observation went this way. "Let us make this analogous to the Sierra Leone situations and experiences in the past, and come up with ideal solutions"

The person simply said, "The solutions are in our hands for we are all in this together"

Another stated the following quite frankly: "As a nation, Sierra Leone can't afford to depend on the West to come to our aid when we experience mosquito bites, suffer from fever, malaria. We can't afford to keep asking them to build and equip our hospitals and clinics in our villages"

I asked him my last question which he answered philosophically, which I had suspected he would do."What should we do then as a nation?"

"We have been part and parcel of the problems. Therefore we should be part, if not the kernels of the solutions"

Once more, taking all the answers into account, it is fair to state that the people of Sierra Leone, including the polity face two vital choices. In other words, they are at the crossroads. Their choices and decisions this crossroads are critical to their recovery and the restoration of the country's past glories. They have no choice but to reinvent the prowess for which the world knew them that is, high standards, educative civilization and law abiding values.

These views were buttressed by one senior government official during the Week of Education at the Bintumani Hotel Hall

> "Sierra Leone was known as an inventive nation and receptive to good ideas. Historically, Sierra Leoneans were known as progressive people that are honest to their beliefs and committed to good practices. The reverse or contrary choice is dangerously risky for the future of this nation. That is, should they choose not to reinvent themselves backed by innovation but maintain the status quo ante the consequences will be dire"

Reinvention means giving birth to new ideas and then nurturing and making them grow productively. These are the stark realities that were at the heart of the choice that the proprietors and founders of IAMTECH made almost three decades ago. These realities constitute the rationale behind the founding of IAMTECH. They are enshrined in the new philosophy that educational reinvention means making learning and teaching relevant and suitable for and their environment. Above all it is transient for the realization of human endeavours.

The rationale stipulates that education should be marketable for the communities and trade centeres which schools, colleges, and universities are established to serve. To translate that into a broader context it means that education should serve and fulfill the needs of country and humanity, which is the key thrust of IAMTECH.

I must state that the proprietors of the institution are the prototypes of personalities made of sterner stuffs in every sense of the word. Now and again some people dream achieving certain concrete goals but along the route, they stumble and fall because they are weak personalities.

This is unlike the proprietors and founders of IAMTECH. Against all the odds, they established their invaluable educational project and have demonstrated that with determination, sincerity, hard work, and faith in God, Allah, all is possible in life.

It is true, for one renowned philosopher and thinker from ancient Greece once said this. "Things are only doable when people think, plan and execute their plans. "We may conclude that our plans are after all doable. Otherwise, plans are completed by our actions to succeed, but they may not necessarily make us achieve our goals"

We need a leap of faith in all that we do in order to succeed. It simply means that all things under the sun are only doable and achievable when people think, plan and execute their plans successfully with a leap of faith.

IAMTECH as the new model of education in the twenty-first century has a peculiar motto when one considers the mottos of other educational institutions in the country. With a philosophical flavour, IAMTECH's motto is "For Country and For Humanity" This motto is the source of the founders' inspiration.

When educational provisions or worthiness are assessed comparatively, the key issues of policies, practices, and cultures of the providers come into sharp focus. It is then that one could determine whether their provisions make meaning in the lives of people and society or not that is or whether they resonate with their philosophy. The providers could be governmental, private or a mixture of public and private partnership (PPP) stakeholders in a given society. The outcomes of such assessments will determine whether such provisions constitute what educationalists call the ideal or liberal type of education.

One of the senior staff once observed: "In an ideal society, education should produce the right calibres, cadres with the right skills and qualifications capable of contributing to the socioeconomic development and political stability of nations"

Paraphrasing the views or philosophy of one humanist, the same staff member said: "Education moulds the characters of those who receive it comprehensively so that they can radiate in the lives of their people and in their nations. Above all, the ideal type of education is a public good"

I have now established the context in which the philosophy of the proprietors is regarded and has been developed over the past two and a half decades their enterprise has existed. It refers to the ideal type of tertiary education capable of addressing all the issues of unfairness and injustice. It also emphasizes that education makes a good citizen. Their philosophy affirms that the ideal type of education creates people who obey the laws of the land and respects the views of those around them so as to create social harmony.

# 4

# Unique

The rationale behind the founding of IAMTECH was underpinned by a profound mission that embodies its philosophy. The philosophy is to make a significant difference in the essence of tertiary education in post war Sierra Leone. The reality that dawned on the founders was that should any tertiary education claim that it has made a difference in the country, it should meet certain key criteria. The criteria are wider access or participation, quality, fairness and the relevance of its programmes.

Let us face reality and say things as they are. It is a bitter herb to swallow, but it has to be said that hitherto, the critical values of fairness, equity, quality and relevance were arguably compromised by the founding fathers. This truth is found in the configuration of the nation state of Sierra Leone in the British colonial era.

The social planners of that era created a two tier system in the configuration of the state. This dispensation had wider ramification for socioeconomic development and by extension impacted on the educational system. In terms of access and widening participation, the statistics varied. The numbers of schools in the colony which was the seat of power of the colonial administration surpassed those in the protectorate areas. Even the few schools built in the protectorate suffered grossly from underfunding.

The critical issue of the scarcity of relevant skills and qualifications or programmes has persisted to this day. The fact is that, as in other countries in most of Africa, Sierra Leone seems to be mired in the philosophy that education is only meant to satisfy intrinsic values which is far from correct. In this day and age, progressive nations have come to realize, sometimes the hard way, the new and complex demands placed on education and the job markets.

Education has become a tool, mechanism, a factory, and an industry that produces goods and services for the consumptions of consumers and internationally. In short, education only makes the difference in people's lives when it functions and its productions meet the requirements of industries and factories.

The history of the political background that paints the true picture of the origins of the configuration of the country was on the minds of Paul and Paula before they gave birth to their project. They were conscious of the fact that at the heart of the problems associated with the configuration of the colonial state were the issues of fairness and wider access. Hence they were determined to make a difference.

I must clarify that since the state of Sierra Leone was reconfigured in the postcolonial period and an up to this period successive regimes have invested substantially in education. Massive school buildings have been constructed and the numbers of entrants into higher education have increased considerably.

However, Sierra Leone's situation became more problematic during the civil war. Earlier structures were destroyed and a war torn country is not rebuilt overnight. No matter the good intentions of the political leadership, rebuilding and reconstruction are herculean tasks to say the least.

As I pointed out in the opening chapters, the couple appeared on the innovative stage, eager to make a difference by trying very hard to fill in the gaps, the vacuums. I have to say that based on raw evidence, since its inception in 1991, IAMTECH has provided education on the basis of fairness, justice and equality and wider participation.

It emphasizes inclusiveness and equity at the main campus in Freetown and at all the other learning centres around the country. Throughout the decades the tertiary sector has endured major difficulties which came to the fore during the civil conflict.

The government then did upgrade some colleges and transformed some of them into polytechnics. These are major reforms and innovations but the demands, and pressures on the system indicate that demands have by far surpassed supply, which is why diversification is needed in the form of new universities in the private sector.

The three main universities in existence have been working to resolve these issues. Equally government has increased the subventions and grants-in-aid that are allotted to them. Unfortunately, subventions and grants-in-aid are not enough to solve problems which are as old as the advent of higher education in Sierra Leone.

The new thinking points towards the strengthening of diversification, especially in the private sector where the attentions of the citizenry have focused over the years. The proliferation of private colleges in the country underscores my arguments.

The comparison is obvious for some might ask what impact IAMTECH has made in relation to the problems I have highlighted. The institute has reached out to the hitherto remote areas in order to redress the chronic failings which have generally marred the tertiary sector.

In sharp contrast, the general trend arguably indicates that most tertiary institutions have failed to operate according to the benevolent values I have highlighted above, which IAMTECH has embraced and practiced since its inception.

The question that may arise is simple but provocative, and it is a soul-searching one. Are the failings in the tertiary sector peculiar to Sierra Leone or are they universal? I am constrained to make this vital point, because it is not a badge of honour or a glittering compliment with which one should be proudly associated. Sierra Leone may not be a peculiar case because history has it that these flaws characterize most tertiary educational institutions in most parts of world.

The Caribbean and Latin American states, with their counterparts in the continent of Africa show the same indicators of failings in these regards. Some theorists have attributed these failing of the sector to endemic poverty and disaffection. But wait a minute! Are we not proposing a weak argument or illogical stance in defence of the endemic failings of the sector?

Put otherwise, if that is the point of argument chosen by the defenders to account for the failings of the sector or education generally, including those in Sierra Leone, what about countries like India, Pakistan and Brazil? These are relatively well-to-do countries.

Depending on which national or other economic development indicators one is trying to cite, some regions in Pakistan are in the middle income earning range, whilst countries like India and Brazil are classified by the IMF and World Bank as developed or close to being classified as developed countries.

Yet, despite all their relatively huge national wealth, it is difficult to argue that the type of education they provide for their citizens is the ideal type in the absolute sense. It is not because it is far from being a public good but rather because it is elitist.

It is because education, I mean quality and the ideal type of education, is provided for an exclusive few, a privileged social class. The indicators which justify my claim are in the elite institutions of India, including the prestigious medical and law schools or accounting and administration academies.

Compounded by the malaises of the Indian caste system, generally speaking, inequality is the microcosms of the clouds of despairs that have hung over the provision of education since India and Pakistan separated in 1947. Hence the manner in which it is ill-managed and distributed as a significant tool of social, economic and political empowerment has been marred by unfairness and injustice.

Taking their situations into consideration, one can safely argue that their system of educational provision, including that of their cohorts in other parts of the world, is classed as education for the selected, privileged few. That which they claim to be their ideal type of education is deeply focused on benefiting only the few, rich, political elites and their associates.

The history of higher education in Sierra Leone is well documented. It is an exciting history that has come a long way since 1827. Since that period, Sierra Leone became the first country in Sub-Saharan Africa to have a higher educational institution. Due to its prowess and pedigree, Fourah Bay College, which now operates under the umbrella of the University of Sierra Leone, was dubbed the Athens of West Africa.

A concerned patriotic citizen stock taker would be eager to ask a vital question. What is the verdict? I am open to corrections, but it could be stated that despite all the hype, arguably, the painful fact endures. That is tertiary education has not really served its rightful purpose for the people of Sierra Leone.

Sierra Leone's educational system may have kicked off with amazing success and glittering opportunities but with the passage of time, it floundered. It is crawling painfully in order to justify its existence. And I say this painstakingly, because the malaises that characterize education have endured for ages now and can't be attributed to a particular political party or government per se. The historical existence of higher education in the land could be deemed as long and fruitless and it has had little impact on the socioeconomic development of the country.

That Sierra Leone still imports experts to teach institutions how to improve reading and writing in our schools is testimony to the failings of the sector. Sierra Leoneans living at home or abroad can't afford to conceal and relish the failings in the name of recent events or calamities anymore.

Sierra Leoneans continue to go down that route, have said Afro centric analysts with the contentious arguments surrounding the endemic poverty of the African continent. They posit that the Trans-Atlantic slave trade is the only causal factor for the enduring poverty and degradation in Africa.

Sierra Leoneans can't afford to advance the civil war, the Ebola epidemic and the floods as the main causes the continuing decline in the standards of education. By the same token, on the political front, we can't afford to take comfort in the usual blame culture. It is pointless to continue blaming a particular government or political party for the enduring failings in the education sector.

I know that you would like to ask-who is to blame. Recall the apt and witty adage that our faults are not in our stars but in ourselves. All Sierra Leoneans are culpable, and so they should all carry the can, and rather respond to the emerging wakeup call! We must realize that our fate and our destiny lies in our hands not in bad omens!

Whilst all Sierra Leoneans yearn for the outcomes of our fate and destiny, let us reflect soberly. Over the decades the failings of education have been associated with several factors. They are the vices no one wants to talk about because they have damaged the country in several ways.

They have disabled and undermined the dreams and values of the ideal type of higher education which most progressives around the world crave for. Had the agents of these endemic vices not hampered this dreamed of ideal type Sierra Leone would have had a system of education that works for all its citizens.

I have to also comment on this key factor as I go along. The agents or causal factors that have been at work for all the failed decades are found in the politics of tribalism, bribery, corruption, and nepotism. In other words, these vices have been at the heart of the debates over why our educational institutions, as well as other national institutions have failed to measure up and meet their goals and objectives as planned by some of the Founding Fathers and even some of those patriots who have steered the ship of state.

Deliberately politicized with contempt, the good intentions of the some of the Founding Fathers and some meaningful patriots have been grossly undermined by some greedy, selfish people in positions of power. This has been the case for the past decades. Many other contentious reasons could be cited for the endemic failings.

However, the vices of bribery, corruption, nepotism and favouritism count as the active agents, the dangerous causal factors. They are the most explosive and powerful, influences to the extent that they have constituted the culture and the acceptable norms in the system. Take it or leave it, but to a large extent, they signify the contrast between the roots of Sierra Leone's failings and the success stories which other nations have built over the years.

Any solution! Solutions could be farfetched, but a proactive and sincere stocktaking is required for the good of the nation. Coming up with makeshifts policy initiatives that are not thought through properly, in order to yield success, is not the way forward, nor is it the best approach to redress the endemic culture of failures within the system.

In his paper presented at the Miata Conference Centre during the launching of the Week of Education 2015, the author observed among other things: "The three causal factors responsible for the enduring malaises in the system include the polity, family and educational institutions. They are all key stakeholders, which is the main reason they should embark on proactive actions as the effective and ideal tools of redress"

Frankly speaking, in order to find a cure for this endemic disease, a comprehensive assessment has to be conducted sooner rather than later. It is the prognosis of the assessment that will determine the kind of cure the system requires.

One of the other presenters at the Miata Conference Centre made another salient point which could be utilized to solve the lingering rots in the system: "We can't afford to proverbially plait the hair on top of lice. We have to venture to the bottom, investigate, identify the filths and eradicate them once and for all"

The endemic failings point at one other related hazard. It is the lack of respect for the values of liberal democracy. Generally speaking, in nations where democracy works at its very best, education is meant to fulfil hosts of socioeconomic needs. Liberally structured and managed education is capable of redressing social, economic and political problems.

When people acquire the liberal type they perform multidimensional functions. They have the capability to prepare people not just to perform an educational role in society. They are meant to prepare reliable, dedicated citizens who will serve positive, receptive, nationalist roles as well as inculcate the values of committed patriotism.

At the school level in wealthy industrialized democratic countries, for example, schooling is expected to produce young people who can enter the labour market with the necessary skills in literacy, computation, and written expressions.

These skills are transient. By transient I mean that they are transferable skills which will be of value to young people and of course adults in other spheres of life. There are many advantages associated with skills that are transferable. They are not limited to one situation or circumstance of successful individuals.

For instance these skills are not only suited to one occupation or profession. Successful candidates have the opportunity to become versatile and competent enough to seek jobs in various occupations. An education system which imparts skills and qualifications containing competences as invaluable as the ones mentioned is dynamic.

One other beauty and benefit about liberal education is that it makes the difference in the lives of not only those who are educated but society at large. It inspires diverse expectations and demands in relation to those who acquire it successfully, especially at the tertiary level. The beneficiaries could be local subsistence farmers, local tradesmen and women, local community leaders and workers.

This is true of the provisions at IAMTECH because the competences of the skills they offer are dynamic. These competences are a lot more expected of their students who successfully complete their courses. And true to their credit, there is a glaring statistic which testifies that students who have passed through IAMTECH have successfully put their skills to work with distinction wherever they have found themselves.

Above all they have made huge impression on communities and the nation. Be these skills sophisticated, practical or theoretical, successful graduates from IAMTECH stand in good stead to serve their compatriots in high society as well as those in the ghettos or disadvantaged communities.

In the wealthy, technologically advanced countries, it is incumbent on further and higher education including colleges, universities, and professional training institutions to produce competent, dynamic and refined people, especially young people, who are deemed to be the successors of the older generations. They the young and refined adults that are been equipped with the necessary and vital skills, knowledge, and qualifications are expected to play responsible roles for the good of society.

It is required of them to perform with distinctions in their various stations of life. They could become productive and successful scientists, experts, and leaders in the various institutions of their society. They can't afford to become self-centred and selfish otherwise, the society that educated them stands to suffer the most.

Education with a difference is also meant to mould the characters, behaviours and attitudes of individuals. It teaches good citizenship. When educational institutions meet these expectations, then they are deemed to have performed their functions as positive facilitators of progress in society. As positive social, civic, and political facilitators they will have made a huge difference in redressing the diverse problems of their country.

As long as educational institutions perform the functions highlighted above, then it would be ideal to class them the new model that makes the difference in the lives of humanity and country. They deserve to be classed as the ideal and liberal type with a difference.

This is undoubtedly the case because such institutions have the capability to produce successful graduates with the viable skills and qualifications the country needs for national development. In hindsight, IAMTECH may have existed for only two and half decades. Yet it has fulfilled most of the criteria which define the ideal, liberal type of education that makes the difference.

# PART TWO

# 5

# Multidimensional Strings

I have repeatedly stated that the ideal type of tertiary education that progressive nations yearn for these days is the type that serves country and humanity. The core values of the ideal type of education are akin to the values of liberalism. Service to country and humanity underscores core liberal values.

We are very much aware these days that education has become a commodity very much associated with commercial and financial values. But there are other values which education should espouse and bring to the fore of human endeavours and aspirations. They are the enviable values to serve country and humanity because educational practices can't endure apart from people and their communities.

By implication or design, the reality of these assertions was heralded before the nation its international partners and distinguished Sierra Leoneans. At the official launching ceremony of the Week of Education 2015, at the Miata Conference Centre, the president, Dr Ernest Bai Koroma echoed these assertions in his keynote address.

The president clearly set out his vision, his plan for the future of education in the country. The eleven-point plan was both comprehensive and ideal for all the reasons I have pointed out in the other chapters. In his eleven point plan, he put forward among other things:

1.  Greater attention to the basics of reading, writing and number work

2.  Ensure a minimum standard for institutions at all levels

3.  Incentive for institutions to do well through a performance based system

4. Ensure the quality of service for teachers by appointing a competent educationalist

5. Ensure trained and qualified teachers are recruited and are on payroll

6. Embark on large-scale teacher improvement programme

7. Provide teaching and learning materials for all government and government assisted institutions at all levels

8. Construct, furnish and provide additional classrooms

9. Explore innovation and alternatives that will allow textbooks and reference materials for teachers

10. Maintain an Inspectorate that will be transformed into a quality inspectorate and learners

11. Encourage quality research

In addition to the eleven point plan, President Koroma acknowledged the huge costs involved in reinventing the quality education the country requires. However, he emphasized that "until we improve in our human capacity we cannot realize the kind of reform that we want to experience in this country"

Significantly the grand historic successes that Sierra Leone's education sector achieved in the glorious past have not lost on President Koroma. In that context he urged the participants and all Sierra Leoneans across the length and breadth of the country to debate the issues sincerely and frankly, come up with solutions and restore the sector to its past glories.

Thus, he said among other things "This will be the foundation, on which we can build to reform education and restore Sierra Leone to its former enviable status" (as noted earlier "the Athens of West Africa")

History attests that nation states have become great by investing in skills and infrastructures, an ideal relished and practiced by the new model of education employed by IAMTECH. The capital projects which the college has undertaken over the years and continues to review, underscore the fact that they believe in this philosophy.

In line with the admission of the president in his keynote address on that day at the Miata Conference Centre, IAMTECH appreciates the fact that there are failings in the sector. Therefore it calls for urgent tangible reforms. For instance, there is this perspective that the educated person skilfully masters and memorizes theories and acquires colourful paper qualifications as the ultimate goal.

That is not the case anymore. The new model, which is all about the ideal type, stresses relevance, and an all-embracing type, which combines the mastering of theory and practical skills and their appropriate applicability for social and economic and spiritual development.

The ideal type brings other values that are also ideal catalysts for human and community success and progress. This is where the inner thought teaches sober reflections. The reflections emphasize that the ideal type of education is one that only has theoretical and practical benefits.

As added values, the ideal types are multidimensional in their totality. The values of the ideal type of education are synonymous with the tasks of factories and industries. They are built for the production of moral and ethical values. These values are not lost on the stakeholders of IAMTECH.

The ethical and moral considerations emphasize good, positive attitudes, behaviours and character which ensure the progress of society. Such institutions are perceived as producers and espousers of the values of success achieved through hard work and determination. They mould students to be polite respectful and honest law abiding citizens.

For in the spirit of good citizenship are found the values of functional and moral education. Citizens who acquire these values are ever ready to face the hard choices and challenges of preserving quality education by maintaining standards through honest and decent professional practices. Citizens educated in that context are ever ready and well-equipped to meet the demands of the twenty-first century competitive labour markets. They are the effective, functional, good citizens required for building a healthy and progressive nation.

Considering all these prerequisites and ideals, the new type of education that nation states require should be holistic both in outlook and in the nurturing and harnessing of productive and beneficial life chances. Those who pursue it can hardly find themselves social misfits in civilized societies.

Education is all about empowerment. The holistic type of education espouses values which are empowering and inclusive in real terms. There is much more to its holistic nature and complexity. At the central to the values of the holistic type of education is inclusiveness through wider participation and receptiveness.

How are the values of the holistic and ideal type of education articulated and achieved, you may ask? In an ideal society it is incumbent on all the stakeholders of education to establish necessary structures which articulate holistic, all embracing values. This means that the polity, the family, and the providers or proprietors together need to establish the necessary structures which guarantee the attainment of defined goals that will create and enhance national cohesion and socioeconomic success.

The custodians of the structures of the ideal and holistic type of education have a heavy load on their shoulders. They will only be deemed useful and successful stakeholders when they take into account all the needs of their clients or students within and beyond the communities they serve.

To reiterate, it is a herculean task. It is incumbent on them to accomplish the tasks for which they were established or the tasks they chose to fulfil. In brief, they must fulfil the aspirations of society through functional and efficient structures. Only then will the structures or agencies be deemed successful entities through which national success will be articulated and realized fully.

I have mentioned the concept of inclusiveness because of its liberal values and connotations. Education in its entirety is a public good and therefore it should be permissive of inclusiveness. It should be designed to serve members of the public and society at large, not a hand-picked few elites. It should not be a private good or ownership at the expense of the disaffected majority. To repeat, this model is obviously found in societies with liberal tendencies. And the providers, especially in the private sector, should have liberal dispositions.

These characteristics and descriptions of the ideal and holistic model in my view, contrast with the exclusive model practiced in other countries. In those countries, it is unfortunate that educational institutions behave as exclusive entities. They are structured and managed in such a way as to serve the needs of the wealthy few and political class.

Coming back to the point, the ideal type of education is the liberal type because it has a human face. It teaches humanist values, virtues and ideals. And this is the significant point about the all-inclusive, liberal, holistic and ideal type of education that IAMTECH offers.

There is one important fact we also need to bear in mind. When one assesses and applies the positive values highlighted to the curricula contents of the programmes at IAMTECH, one arrives at one important conclusion. Above all, it serves the needs of country and humanity. Hence it is the cornerstone of both the motto and philosophy of the institution as stated inter alia.

I am constrained to conclude this chapter with two critical questions. Compare and contrast the values of the ideal and holistic type of higher education at IAMTECH (the new model) and the values and ideals of the other examples around the world that I have pointed out in the preceding chapters. Ask yourself these two critical questions. Do they serve country and humanity? Do they serve the demands, needs and aspirations of the twenty-first century competitive job markets?

# 6

# Reckoning Force

There are many questions that might spring to the minds of the critics when they realize that I have decided to give a lot more credence to the Institute of Advanced Management and Technology in this book. (IAMTECH) For example they might ask: In the general sense, can we convincingly argue that the courses offered by IAMTECH have contributed significantly to the socioeconomic development of Sierra Leone? Has this college actually made any significant difference since its inception?

There is an English proverb which states that the sweetness of the pudding is in the eating. Undoubtedly, the institute has proved its mettle in many significant ways. Indeed it has had its fair shares of challenges, like all other sister institutions in the land. However, it has pulled through successfully. The country's Ministry of Trade and Labour can attest to the claim that IAMTECH is a force to reckon with in terms of its substantial contributions to the socioeconomic development of Sierra Leone through its versatile diligent, qualified, and efficient products.

And to buttress further this is why. My assertions find support in the fact that most of those who go through IAMTECH secure gainful employment in strategic sectors of the nation's economy. IAMTECH's former students are found in the public as well as private sectors where they have held their own in senior managerial or directorship positions.

Far from those days when the values of education only meant a piece of paper qualifications, IAMTECH values a system of education that is akin to the one that modernism requires for socioeconomic advancement. These values are all found in the methods and philosophy of the ideal type of practices and policies for which IAMTECH is renowned. To reiterate it is the ideal type of education that all Sierra Leoneans seek and yearn for at a critical time when the nation's economy has been hit by unforeseeable national tragedies the aftermaths of the devastating civil war, followed in 2014 and 2015 by the Ebola epidemic and destructive floods.

Decades have come and gone and questions are being asked about the overall performance of the education system. The questions are centered on the fact that some form of concrete action should be taken. The populace continues to clamour that the polity should reform the system and restructure it to the ideal type of education. The new type they would like to see emerge is one that will break all the unhealthy barriers, eliminate the entrenched dependency culture and reconfigure a liberal society.

The populace are relentless in their demands which are of course legitimate for they cherish a nation and society that believes in the acquisition of knowledge and the inculcation of values which create the equitable redistribution of wealth. Hence, patriotic Sierra Leoneans not only cherish this ideal but they also work round the clock in order that educational institutions teach the right skills and qualifications which in the final analysis produce graduates adequately equipped to meet the essential needs of each and every person in society.

The acquisition of such a model of education, they sincerely believe, empowers and seals the common destiny of country and humanity. These values constitute the eleven points which define the type of renewed education system that President Koroma envisages for Sierra Leone.

The president's open acknowledgement that IAMTECH's provisions earn its graduates lucrative jobs in the country underscores the significant points I have made all along. The institution's ideal type of education is versatile in its impacts and functions. Besides maximising socioeconomic development, by implication it ensures political stability as well. When the economies of nations are healthy, the potentials for political stability are more likely than ever.

Educationalists and their associate professionals are firmly united in this opinion. That is in societies where youths are trained, educated in vital skills, and empowered to secure gainful employment, more often than not, political stability will be assured. The logic is simple when their energies are harnessed and utilized in profitable ways, they will be kept off the streets and also kept away from trouble. The saying goes that an idle mind is troubled, restless and apt to offend the laws of the land. How often have we heard of jobless young people caught up in violence and crimes?

Training people in vital transferable skills is ideal but it is not the only requirements for national development and political stability. Sierra Leone like most less developed countries needs an educational system with moral and ethical bents.

The acquisition of needed skills is vital for economic development but skills are irrelevant without good behaviours. Good behaviour and positive character backed by relevant education couched in strong national character as tangible, binding values create a functional and useful workforce for any progressive nation.

Alumni and alumnae oriented in these values are apt to move in the same progressive directions. They are bonded by the simple logic that espouses the sharing of a common destiny. This will earn them the gateway to accelerated economic growth and success cemented by social cohesion and national unity.

One of the heads of department (HOD) at IAMTECH puts it cleverly and logically: "That which binds us together as a progressive nation articulates the present as well as the future destinies of all Sierra Leoneans. It is this reality that constitutes the cornerstones of the values of the programmes we offer here at IAMTECH"

The micro and macro functions of an ideal type of education are even more ideal for a country like Sierra Leone. A country like ours emerging from terrible warfare, compounded by the ravages of the Ebola virus and the recent floods does not need a one dimensional education. That is the curricula should be reviewed regularly to keep up with the changing times. Teaching old skills and offering outdated courses can only be bad for individual as well as national development.

It has to be also said that for far too long, most Third World countries have wallowed in the wrong belief that education, especially higher education should be provided by the government and its agents. We live in a world that places more demands and strains on governments and the public sector. So there is now an alternative, or a model which professes a collaborative approach. The government or public and the private sectors should work in the spirit of partnership and corporation. It is credible at that.

The public-private partnership (PPP) model should take a preeminent place, especially in Sierra Leone's tertiary sector. This brings us to the relevance of the diversification model as a progressive educational strategy. It has been too long in coming and now the wait should be seen to be over in real, practical terms.

There should be no compromise over the wholesale implementation of this model in the tertiary sector because post-war, post Ebola, and post-flooding Sierra Leone needs a model of education that is functionally dynamic and encourages diversification. This ideal sustains the points made before. The theory or logic of the common destiny of Sierra Leoneans "hang on strings" that harness all the diverse entities of which they are composed as a nation. A united, collaborative approach that adopts interdisciplinary studies and keeps abreast of the times should be essential elements to any new curriculum or curriculum reviews.

In brief, the public private partnership model is ideal for our situation because education can't perform effectively and productively in isolation. It has to encourage inclusiveness and diversification with all hands on deck. Therefore, community engagements and supports as practiced at IAMTECH are vital for the success of such a model.

Most significantly, despite the efforts of the government, the country's economy has been unfortunately reduced to mere existence. This is because the contributions of the tertiary sector of our national education system have been minimal. Worse, even those minimal gains over the decades have not been fully maximized and utilized effectively for the common good.

It is painful to remind ourselves of these salient points, but they will serve as corrective measures for the country's renewal. The country's economy had nearly recovered when the deadly Ebola epidemic and floods struck. These national hazards had a debilitating socioeconomic impact on the national economy and development. Even now that Ebola has been defeated all indications are that it will take decades for what has been reduced to a fragile economy to recover fully and sporadically.

National consciousness is the most important enabling instrument that will ensure that the efforts of the national recovery and wealth generation plan which the government has put in place will be fully realized. Sierra Leone has come a long way and has had rough patches. One would have thought that those rough times would have taught Sierra Leoneans vital lessons by now. They could have learned from them and made lasting amends. Unfortunately that has not proved to be the case. What the nation needs now is to embrace solutions which are informed by significant ideals.

Only when governments and their social planners themselves learn from these lessons which have been carelessly ignored will the tertiary sector record the massive success for which this nation thirsts. In addition, the nation's social planners in particular need to recognize that education only becomes an effective tool for socioeconomic development when it serves micro and macro roles and functions.

In its bid to serve these roles effectively, the tertiary sector needs key facilitating synergies. These synergies hang on several holistic strings which social planners can't afford to ignore at this critical time of the nation's history. They are holistic strings which require inclusiveness and diversification of the tertiary tier. When successfully planned, formulated and executed, they will supply the answers to Sierra Leone's short as well as long term problems.

Substantial efforts should be made by social planners and other important stakeholders in the education sector to eliminate the physical as well as policy barriers to diversification. The legacies of the old bottleneck problems which debarred the progress of many aspirants to pursue higher education still endure in most places. It is only through proactive policy initiatives that these barriers and handicaps can be eliminated once and for all.

By removing these barriers the government sector will have created a level playing field for all individual aspirants (investors) and aspiring institutions, still waiting patiently in the queue to operate on the same stage as the rest of society. It is no longer an option to preserve the so-called integrity which now wallows in the shadows.

The Tertiary Education Commission (TEC) has put in a lot of effort and continues to do so in order to manage carefully and successfully the growing aspirants in the public sector and secure quality assurance. The commission is quite explicit in its administration of the sector. That is they deem that private providers should be encouraged to operate only if they meet the criteria stipulated by the constitution of the land.

The social planners and their associate stakeholders should recognize this vital point. The TEC needs more financial and logistical support to actualize its massive, meaningful efforts and duties. It should be reiterated that it needs concrete financial and logistical support, in addition to the substantial aid of government, to enable it to create a sector capable of meeting the nation's needs.

Again, making inclusivity and diversity part and parcel of the social planers' priorities will kick-start some of the key issues that were discussed at the Miata Conference Centre during the Week of Education, 2015. The period of redemption, renewal, and restoration of the past glories of Sierra Leone's educational system and the preservation of national pride is now!

Now is the time for the polity, family and educational institutions (all stakeholders) to step up to the plate and do that which is right in the name of country and humanity. The social planners can no longer afford to create a false sense of relevance and security in this vital facet of national renewal. Doing so will amount to painting a picture of beautiful feathers. Superficially, they will be painting the picture of a sector that looks externally beautiful but is internally rotten.

# 7

# Strange Paradox

Amongst the critics and analysts, some harbour a strange paradox. It is suspiciously tied to the failures of education in Sierra Leone, especially the tertiary sector. Amazingly, this paradox unleashes an interesting catch 22scenario. The paradox is centered on the argument that the persistent endemic failings in the system should be perceived as a huge blessing in disguise.

What they are saying is simply that the enduring failings in education have amazingly led to unthinkable advantages which could help correct the nation's chronic, stubborn errors. Some have even hinted that had these errors not been exposed the nation would have continued to bask in a false sense of success and security.

The analysts of this school of thought point to a series of examples in the sector to underscore their arguments. A typical case in point is the proliferation of tertiary institutions in the private sector. However, the Ministry of Education Science and Technology and professionals need to consider closely the vital issue of the inherent flaws associated with the quality of teaching and learning resources. The professionals and experts at the MEST should examine the pedagogy taught to trainee teachers and lecturers at their various teacher training colleges. These are the malaises which have blighted the sector for decades now and they have gone unchecked. They militate against the preservation of quality and the raising of standards at all the tiers which constitute the sector.

The good news is that these vital issues are not only on the lips of every Sierra Leonean, they have become unbearable to the extent that they have inspired serious debates. National consciousness has been invoked and the populace will not rest until the necessary measures are taken to resolve the enduring problems.

Some of the newly established colleges are less equipped, due to the lack of funding and government subventions. And the responsibility is not limited to any particular political party or government.

A concerned citizen summed it up sensibly:

> "The enduring failures in our educational institutions should not be allotted to politics and politicians alone. They are not about particular governments. The issue of some private colleges and universities not making the grades is not due to lapses at the TEC either. The problems have to do with lack of care amongst the very people of this land. Those who operate private institutions should bear the blame if their colleges or schools are not living to expectations. So are the public, elite institutions. Those who are running them should bear the brunt, not government or any particular political party. The fact is that neither governments nor political parties can police everything in the land. Citizens ought to take direct responsibility for the good of the country. That is what good and responsible citizenship is all about. It is about looking after the interest of the state and its institutions. They should not be left entirely to the whims and caprices of politicians."

Quality assurance and standards have become the unfortunate casualties of the proliferation of private colleges. The same could be said of the elite higher educational institutions.

The above quoted views of that concerned citizen make absolute sense. But by the same token, governments, their stakeholders and institutions should become part and parcel of the coalition of the determined and responsible citizens and redress the problems of the nation.

By the government's own admission the sector needs proactive if not revolutionary strategies in order to curb the malpractices which prevail in the education sector. The revelations inspired by the critical analysis presented by the experts at the Miata Conference Centre and Bintumani

Hotel Hall on those fateful days reached the conclusions on the minds of the populace.

They have given the nation hope that change and realistic reforms of the sector are imminent. They also assured the nation that the polity and her agencies are determined now, more than ever before, to clean up this all important ambit of the state apparatuses at all cost.

IAMTECH and its founders, as well as the entire administration and faculty are gratified for the help government has made available to the institution. However, it is reasonable to state one vital point. Considering the sporadic rate of inflation and the weight of the capital projects the institution has undertaken, such as adequate classroom facilities, libraries and laboratories only one thing can see these vital projects through.

Substantial funding and subventions are required. In addition, diversification through the running of learning centeres outside the Freetown headquarters of the institution is a necessary development strategy. This innovative strategy requires substantial financial and logistical interventions from government, charitable organizations and well-wishers.

IAMTECH needs substantial capital to continue to preserve quality assurance and fruitfully ensure the policy of diversification. This is a crucial and benevolent policy that the institution has ever relished as one of the cornerstones of its philosophy since its inception.

The government should "invest massively in skills and infrastructure, then the nation will prosper" Thankfully this ideal or progressive philosophy was echoed by President Koroma in his keynote address at the Miata Conference Centre during the Week of Education 2015.

I urgently need to clarify a particular point. Private colleges and schools are not the problems that have marred the sector. Put otherwise, the flaws that have been identified as stubborn thorns in the flesh of the sector are not limited to institutions in the private sector. In fact the advent of private institutions in post war Sierra Leone has helped the sector and the country at large in many ways. They have eased the prevailing bottleneck culture that marred the system in the past when candidates had to drop out due to the inadequate places at the only two elite institutions in the country.

The operation of polytechnics along with private tertiary colleges suits the overall national development philosophy of the previous government as well as the current one.

They formulate, and above all, endorse the vital clauses which describe the public-private partnership initiatives. They are economically beneficial and benevolent blueprints, which pages were borrowed or taken from the Third Way economic philosophy and development policy of the former New Labour Party Prime Minister Tony Blair.

What should be of important concern for governments and the populace is the efficient management of quality assurance, public elite institutions or private tertiary institutions notwithstanding! Thankfully these vital issues have not escaped the attention of IAMTECH. Hence they constitute the very live wires and lynchpins of the massive success stories the institution has built over the past two and a half decades.

Relevance of the curriculum contents and the performances and contributions of the recipients of the skills they teach are equally assured. IAMTECH fits these bills due to its amazing track record. This institution has amazingly performed as a private provider with a difference in the history of private tertiary education in post war Sierra Leone.

Time has passed and history has been made, which will be enshrined in the history of IAMTECH. It has gone a long way since its inception in 1991 in ensuring that it justifies its existence and philosophy of private provisions.

It was founded as a small computer training institute in the outskirts of the city of Freetown in Kissy in 1991. Little did the founders know that it would be one of the leading architects leading the way for the renewal of standards, relevance in programmes and excellence in the tertiary sector in post war Sierra Leone!

It has to be said that smart and innovative as they are, the founders were quick to identify and understand the weaknesses in the country's tertiary sector. Upon reflection, this private tertiary institution has created a sharp contrast between its provisions and the rest of the tertiary sector.

*Dr. Michael Nicolas Wundah*

I must repeat that my analysis should not be misconstrued as casting aspersions on governments now and then for allowing the failings in the sector to persist for decades now. Rather the failings belong to all Sierra Leoneans. As a matter of fact successive governments have recognized the fact that there are enduring, chronic widespread failings in the system.

The fall in standards is an open secret in Sierra Leone. On numerous occasions, the media as well as politicians, especially policy-makers at the Ministry of Education Science and Technology (MEST), have made their views and anguish known.

The problems were brought to the fore, as stated inter alia during the recent Week of Education inaugural and celebrations across the length and breadth of the country, the chief education officer, Dr Mohamed Alhaji Kamara was very explicit and expressed his determination to clean up the system. The government is determined to combat fraud and corruption in the education sector just as it is determined to do the same in all facets of society.

To back up the government and ministry's dissatisfactions and the stance it is determined to adopt the CEO made it explicit in the well written and uncompromising paper he presented on that day. His stern position spelt out a singular voice and message "those who corrupt the education sector will face the wrath of justice".

I listened carefully and attentively to the uncompromising tone of the chief education officer at the ministry not as a passive participant but as a presenter of one of the symposium papers. I also served as chairman of the occasion, alongside Mr Horatio Modupeh Nelson-Williams, the executive secretary at the MEST.

I have reproduced some important passages and pointers of his seminar paper below. I have to reiterate that the chief education officer took pains to make these salient points.

Describing the spate of corruption in the system, he said: "Corruption in my view is the use of public office for private gain. In other words, this could refer to the use of one's office, position, rank or status for his/her own personal benefit that could be earned through bribery, extortion,

48

fraud, embezzlement, nepotism, influence peddling etc, all of which can be categorized as activities of corruption".

He stressed the wider ramifications of gross malpractices in the sector, including corruption: "I must therefore hasten to mention that any sector of a society, which in its operations is associated with any or a combination of these activities, is sure to be faced with challenges that could result in development impediments"

He identified specific malpractices that have undermined the integrity of the education sector: "In the education sector of this country, the engagement of some of our stakeholders in some of these corrupt practices is no hidden secret as the manner in which they are widely perpetrated seems to portray them as accepted norm and over the years, eating into and destroying the quality of our education"

In order to assure the nation that all was not lost, he affirmed among other things the following:

"Finally, I want to leave you with the assurance that our education legal documents that is our policies, acts and other related documents are absolutely enough to guide us on the dos and do nots within the education sector. If we religiously follow what their contents say we will surely operate a corruption free education system in this country and produce students with the quality of education that will earn them excellent and credible qualifications for enhanced competitiveness in the global market"

I have chosen to conclude this chapter from the view-points of IAMTECH's humanist philosophy and ideology. It is the mantra of the liberal values I have referred to extensively in this and previous chapters of this book.

I would say without any reservation that as the humanists they truly are, the proprietors and founders of IAMTECH have manifested key values of the ideal type of education. These values include the eradication of all the malpractices highlighted by the acting chief education officer, which I have quoted above.

Above all, the proprietors are renowned for condemning these malpractices at all times within and beyond the walls of the college. Above all, the message is cemented in the minds of students and further in black and white official documents. They are boldly enshrined in the contracts which govern the relationship between the students and IAMTECH.

They constitute the policy blueprints of the college. The founding couples stand for the practice of ethical and moral values in the system at all times. They truly do, for they believe that these values are the cornerstones of the philosophy and ideology of the educational system of any progressive nation.

According to humanists and liberal educationists and philosophers, including Rousseau, the policies and the strategies of the ideal type of education are invaluable learning enablers. They cater to all and sundry, regardless of inherent differences in orientation.

The proprietors of this college are liberal minded humanists. And as the cliché goes, liberal minded people think and behave liberally. That is the reason why Paul and his supportive wife believe that Sierra Leone needs the liberal, ideal type of tertiary education affirming that it should encourage access and wider participation because it is a public good.

It is the only assurance needed to redeem the positive values that some of the well-meaning founding fathers of the educational system in Sierra Leone had in mind. They were the indigenous nationalists, educationists, politicians and social activists. The fact that these likeminded couples in this day and age in Sierra Leone believe in the same values and philosophy, their story should be recorded for the sake of posterity.

# PART THREE

# 8

# Memory Lane

A bosom friend and relative of Paul and Paula, Dr Bob Seasay, spoke highly about their diligence, industry, honesty, and determination. These are values which they have utilized to great effect over the decades to serve their country and humanity.

# 9

# Students Voices

There is a very wise saying which states that without pupils establishing educational institutions is unnecessary. It will prove futile. The inherent logic of this wise saying is relevant to the rich narratives of this book which encompass multiple opinions.

---

It is important that this logic affirms that in an educational setting, students matter very much, just as the massive structures as well as the academicians who lecture, train and develop them. It is as a result of this undisputed fact on my mind that I have included the candid opinions and willing voices of past and present students of IAMTECH in this book.

But they are not the only glittering, convincing, unbending voices. Equally, I have solicited the opinions of a cross section of members of staff at IAMTECH. Their voices are vital for the rich values which underpin the founding and fruitful existence of IAMTECH as one of the standards bearers in the tertiary sector.

---

The ethnic demographics of the college represent the exceptionally receptive ethnic dimensions of Sierra Leone.

One former student union president of the college once said: "The beautiful colourful nature of the college is found in its poly ethnicities. The age and social differentials also typify a carbon copy of Sierra Leone's social and cultural complexities. The college is highly respected for its religious tolerance, which is one of the country's greatest strengths"

There is something beneath the surface of this admirable national resemblance which the college proudly bears with the country. However, I have to make a passing comment on this unique national characteristic aspect of Sierra Leone's glittering values in context. It goes deeper than we see on paper or on the lips of the people themselves, including their politicians.

Undoubtedly Sierra Leoneans pride themselves on a liberal, religious and ethnic tolerance and interregional cohesion. It means that it is a multicultural society in the atmosphere of peace and reconciliation. Yet, beneath the surface of this calm, receptivity there is a benign reality. In the eyes of critical analysts this picture of a beautiful picturesque Sierra Leone with multicultural values and bereft of tribalism could be reduced to a mirage.

Historically this is why. The country's hidden, regional divisions are often ignited by ethnic feuds over the unhealthy, corrupt competitions for the shares of the national wealth. At the centre of these feuds are some greedy politicians. The good news is that these ill habits and vices are not tolerated by students and general staff at this college.

More significant in my view is a sobering piece of advice for our social planners and their allied stakeholders. Perhaps the country's social planers and policymakers should take a page from the ethos of IAMTECH. Some of their strategies and liberal approaches which have held together and successfully created the social cohesion the college and its students enjoy are worth experimenting with in various quarters, facets of our national administration.

The college runs a two shift system with morning and evening sessions. There is a good age mix and the gender composition, which has become a political hot potato in the country, is relatively balanced at IAMTECH. The institution is renowned as a second chance-giver. By this I mean that it offers to students who initially dropped out of college and forgo the opportunity of a second chance return to tertiary education and successful study. It puts them in good stead to land decent, well paid jobs and earn a decent living and contribute positively to their own development as well as national development.

IAMTECH is flexible in most areas of its operations. It applies the same flexibility to its admission policies. Quite recently, it did the same during and after the national catastrophes the Ebola epidemic and flooding.

At those critical times this flexibility was reflected in the timetabling of examinations and re-sit examinations. Special concessions were granted to students deemed to be vulnerable and incapacitated.

To reiterate, the flood hit the western area of the city unfortunately during examinations week. Students living in the flooded areas as well as learning centeres located near them were granted due concessions to take their papers at suitable times.

This does not in any way suggest that IAMTECH encourages watering down academic standards. I have stated repeatedly in previous chapters the strictures and the preservations of quality assurance as dear to the hearts of the administrators. Maintaining standards is one of the many cornerstones of the ideals and policies of the college. IAMTECH applies these measures rigorously in order to preserve high standards and accelerate academic achievements.

And the institute stands out looking over the shoulders of others whenever comparisons are made in these regards. It is clearly evident that the records of the college compare favourably to those of other institution. It is renowned for maintaining high standards in the country. While cases of scandals for examination malpractices have affected the integrity and credibility of other institutions, IAMTECH has never been accused of such malpractices since its inception. No print, electronic or airwaves media outfits has ever accused the college of examinations malpractices.

The civil war has taught Sierra Leoneans some vital lessons. Some of them are about racial and ethnic tolerance and receptiveness. The college admits students unto its programmes from all walks of life and there is an excellent gender, social, political, and religious tolerance. There are students from all faiths and religious backgrounds, including Muslims, Christians and Hindus.

It is an important tradition of the institution to admonish, correct and direct students during matriculations on these important matters as part and parcel of its policies. At the beginning and end of each term, town hall type meetings, they are called by the Americans are conducted. At these important meetings the senior management, including the principal and vice principals and students use the occasion to discuss vital issues. It is during the boardroom meetings that the senior management explains the rules and regulations of the institution to students.

These meetings combine academic as well as social matters. The speeches are poignant academically, very penetrating and frank. At the end of all the speeches, students are given the floor to ask relevant questions to which answers and clarifications are made by the senior management, lecturers, deans and heads of departments. It is a dialogical tradition which is highly respected and given credence by the senior management and students.

It is the distinct spirits of this tradition that has inspired me to include the voices of the students in the comparative narratives of this book. Without their voices, in my view, this book would be incomplete.

In this context, I have selected a handful of students and lecturers to lend their rich voices. I also have to reveal that some of them asked to remain anonymous and I have respected that wish. Also in order to observe gender balance and equity, I chose four males and four females from the various disciplines and faculties of the institution.

The management department is the largest department, so by virtue of their numerical strength, I gave them the privilege to kick off the exercise. The first male students commented as follows: "I am in the final year of my degree course. I am specializing in management. This is the best institution in this country. We are now a force to reckon with in Sierra Leone. It is no longer a one man show in Sierra Leone. Gone are the days when they recognized only one university in Sierra Leone. IAMTECH is here for good and is capable of competing with the very best anywhere in the modern world"

The second male student was very comprehensive and spoke at length, commenting particularly on the qualities of the entire staff. The venue for the interviews was the college's Abie Paula Amphitheatre. Overseeing the amphitheatre is the six story building undergoing construction. It is one of the capital projects of the college.

The student took a hard look at the massive building that is almost complete and he commenced passionately:

"This is IAMTECH. It is the institution of my choice and I must confess that I am a student of this popular college in Sierra Leone. I look forward to the day, it will be made a university"

> "The stature of this massive building and the contributions of each and every one of you that have impacted on my life so positively will be sorely missed. Please forgive me for I must single out two great people; they are the great founders of this college. Their names will be on the lips of everyone in this land. My Good God shall multiply the blessings of Mr and Mrs Kamara. They have made their family and country extremely proud of their historic contributions!"

Male student number three was very philosophical in his comments-"I am in my first year, and wish to specialize or major in procurement. I have gained immensely from the course already, although I am in my first year. Professor Paul Kamara and his caring and great wife, Dr Abie Paula Kamara are people with great wisdom. We were told during the orientation that this institution started as a computer college at Kissy." Pointing to the massive structures in the compound, he concluded: "Look at these beautiful, massive structures. They will be their legacy of which their children and great grandchildren will ever be proud"

Before we treat ourselves to the contributions or opinions of the three final female students, I must reveal what I gathered from their dispositions and their comments as they I spoke to them. The first and most senior of the three female students was adamant that I must write exactly what she felt about the project.

"I am vocal and you can ask my lecturers in the Technology Department. They will tell you that I say things as they are. What I am about to say is vital and worth reflecting on by the administrators as well as the founders of IAMTECH"

I composed myself to deal adequately with this particular student. By the time she had made known her candid opinion about IAMTECH I realized that she was speaking sincerely from the heart. "Go on and speak your mind young lady!" I urged her.

"I must confess to you that when one of my schoolmates and personal friends tried to convince me to enrol at IAMTECH, I laughed cynically"

"Why did you laugh?"

"Well, I honestly thought at that time that IAMTECH is one of those mushrooms. I was doubtful about the prospect of the success and viability of private tertiary institutions because most of them have failed. They are nothing but money making machines."

"How long have you been here and what degree course are you pursuing?" I asked her.

"I am a third year student in the oil and gas department, sir"

"So do you still harbour any doubts about the institution and the department?"

She shook her head and said firmly, "After three years, I must confess that I have no more doubts about IAMTECH. All I am happy to say right now is that I have enjoyed my course and I am impressed by the lecturers and the entire staff."

"What about the proprietors?"

"I think I have commented on them by implication."

"How did you do that?"

"Well, if the college is doing well, which is the case then the founders must have contributed hugely to the success stories of IAMTECH and that includes the lecturers and administrative staff."

"It means that you have changed your mind regarding the negative opinions you had about this institution in the past?"

She smiled and replied, "Yes of course, and almost all of the students hold this institution in high regard. The founders, lecturers and all who have made things happen here are very efficient and hardworking personnel."

When I turned to her two classmates, they sounded as if they were literally singing from the same hymn sheets. Their sweet hymns sounded nothing other than praises in honour of the things that all the stakeholders of IMATECH have achieved in the last twenty five years.

Their hymn sheets rhymed as follows:

"We are very proud of this college. We have no regrets for studying at this college. By the time we successfully complete our studies, we will be well positioned to demonstrate wherever we choose to go, that we got the best out of a quality tertiary institution."

And reflecting on the founders, their hymns were more harmonious, synchronizing and sweet.

"The founders have made Sierra Leone proud because when we are granted autonomous university status, the whole of Sierra Leone will appreciate the fact that we deserve it and that our contributions to national renewal are second to none in the land"

# 10

# Staff Voices

The opinions of students at IAMTECH are very important as they are the very reasons for the institution's existence. Although the lenses through which their beneficiaries view students and staff members, their views are equally important, so I turned to the staff members. I stand to be corrected, but I believe that members of staff, including lecturers have the ability to assess the relationship between the founders, their students and themselves.

This has been said time and again because of the important message it sends. IAMTECH is traditionally a family, a united force, with ties similar to the tight relationship between benches and nails. And most significantly, all members are deemed worthy stakeholders. In brief, students and teachers or lecturers deserve a special place in the history of the college. Generally, they combine to form the bedrocks of teaching and learning in any school, college or university environment.

Moreover, I was inspired to have the opinions about students and staff members recorded in this book because the proprietors impressed on my mind the special relationship between them, students and members of staff.

When I assumed my role as the Vice Principal Administration at the college in March 2015, they invited me to a special session. The session went quite well. The issues that the proprietors discussed with me were frank, sincere and down-to-earth.

The session lasted for forty to forty five minutes. I often forget many things except those that have direct connection with my hobby and profession, a professional writer and published author. On that occasion, I literally memorized all the issues we discussed due to the lasting impressions they made on my mind.

One of the important issues we discussed that morning was the need to tap into the raw talents of the institution including lecturers and students. Dr Paul bit his lips as he made this particular point and begged me in few words. "Doctor" he said, "these are my people." Then he took a deep breath and continued. "They are not ordinary members of staff to me and my wife they are like our blood relatives. Here at IAMTECH, we are family now and we have bonded together for years, come rain or sunshine."

As I said before, the staff that consented to be interviewed decided to have their personal details kept secret. In no particular order, these are the comments they made, including the "Pa" and the "Mammy", as Paul and Paula are fondly known.

"Tell me a bit about the relationship between you and the founders of this institution," I started my interview with one of the interviewees.

"The others have said all I would have said anyway," the interviewee said.

I smiled and asked him to make his own points and contributions. "If I may ask, first of all tell me, how long have you been in this institution?"

"I have served IAMTECH for close to two decades"

"That is amazing! If I may ask again you started here as what?"

"I came here as a student at the expense of the generosity of the Paul Kamara family"

"Explain that sweet phrase you have used at the expense of the generosity!"

He was very emotional at this point. Almost in tears, he replied, "The founders are generous to a fault. They paid my fees from diploma to degree and then gave me my first job here at IAMTECH"

"Why do you say that they are generous to a fault?"

He could not hold back the tears but spoke through them. "I say so because they can sacrifice their pleasures and happiness for others. Isn't that an act of amazing generosity to a fault? It is only a saint of the highest order that can afford to do that for more often than not, it is a big risk!"

I nodded and affirmed, "Surely, you are right. This is a selfish world we live in. Not many people can afford to sacrifice their own happiness for the benefit of others"

The next lecturer was a female who lectures one of the most popular courses in the social science department. Some of her colleagues call her the machine, due to her hard work. Her dedication to duty could only be defined as one with passion and amazing seriousness. She was on her way to teach one of her classes on that day. She barely agreed to be interviewed at the expense of half an hour of her lecture time.

"Some of your colleagues call you the machine. Why?"

"Well I don't know whether it is a joke or mockery"

"I think they mean it" I assured her.

She was not too comfortable with the first question, so I engaged her from a different angle I knew she would be comfortable with. "What do you think about your proprietors?"

"I want to say sincerely that they are a great family. They have the hearts of gold, generous, compassionate and they are a God-fearing couple"

"Are they inspiring people, what do you think?"

"Obviously, they are. If they were not inspiring people, but just dreamers, would they have developed this successful project that endures to this time?"

She was taking up her files to go and deliver her lecture when I stopped her to clarify something. "I am not sure, but because they have made it doesn't necessarily mean that they are inspiring or even make the attempt to inspire other people like us their members of staff"

She shook her head in utter disagreement and retorted, "I beg to disagree with you on that score"

"Why do you say so?"

"I say so because they always make efforts to inspire other people. They offer scholarships to their staff and some of our students. They also give personal advice to us at all times, especially Paula, the wife"

I smiled and said jokingly, "I am going to put you under the limelight"

"Shoot!" She bluffed.

"Have they personally helped you in any form?"

"They gave me a substantial loan to pay for my postgraduate course for which I remain grateful"

The two staff I have highlighted above lecture morning shift classes. I interviewed two members of the evening shift. They are both females.

"How do you find your career with IAMTECH and what is your personal opinion about Paul and Paula?"

"This is what our students in this part of the world refer to as a pregnant question"

I smiled and said, "I call it a double barrel question"

"Okay, whatever name we call it let me answer your question" She took three steps forward and; leaned on one of the pillars along the stairs of the administrative building. I thought she was in a trance because little did I know that this simple question would impact on her psychologically and emotionally.

She spoke to me with her eyes wide open as if to say *trust what I am going to tell you*. "IAMTECH is a family and the founders are amazing and motivating"

I interrupted. "Everyone calls IAMTECH a family. What do they mean?"

"It means that the founders treat their staff as if we are one family"

"And truly, are you members of staff truly a family?" I asked pointedly.

"I don't only feel so on paper or in theory. We are practically, morally and ethically a family at IAMTECH"

She went on to state enthusiastically. "They encourage everyone here to build and develop our career. I think, and like the rest, our careers are safe in the hands of the founders"

My final lecturer is a relative of Paul and Paula. I chose to interview her so that I might make some clarifications as well as justify the things that have been said about the founders by the other lecturers and even by students.

"You are a relative of the founders of IAMTECH"

"Yes I am proud to be!"

"How do you think they treat other members of staff?"

"They are selfless personalities, who go out of their ways and help people regardless whether they are family or not"

I looked at her meaningfully and asked "How can you justify that generous, blanket statement you've just made about your relatives, the founders?"

She smiled and said, "I'm not mistaken"

"What you mean you're not mistaken?"

"I knew you would treat my statement with some degree of doubt or suspicion"

"Well that it is not my line of thought. However you need to convince me, clear any doubts in my mind!"

She replied with bravado and hit the right note. "Quite recently, my relatives the founders of this great institution paved the way for one of our colleagues in the business department to go to China and study. And many more staff members have benefited from this culture of giving freely by Paul and Paula. I am sure you are aware that sacrificing for others is not common these days in our society"

The amazing thing about the revelations made by both students and staff members in relation to the founders is that they do motivate and inspire their members of staff and students. These facts and assertions have been made bare in the opinions the two groups have offered about them.

The revelations have convinced me to conclude that the success stories of Paul and Paula have been due largely to the positive human relations for which they are renowned. The manners in which they deal with those around them are inspiring. How about giving acres of land to some deserving employees? One of their employees had the opportunity to make the pilgrimage to the Holy land Mecca, if the Ebola epidemic had not hit Sierra Leone.

Their style of management has been very inspiring too. According to the revelations of students and staff, they combine discipline, professionalism and good, inspiring social relationships. That does in my view mean that their social skills, including warmth, interpersonal relationships and discipline have implications for the successful running of organizations.

The founders are profound disciplinarians according to the prevailing evidence and as ascertained by staff and students. These good qualities have undoubtedly boosted the potentials of their project to survive during the difficult times.

IAMTECH has endured many tough challenges throughout the past years because of these sparkling, positive humane qualities of the founders. Their college has continued to grow and prosper due to the qualities they, the founders and those who work for them have profoundly manifested in the relationships between them, their students and the society they serve.

# PART FOUR

# 11

# Benevolent Pioneers

One philosopher reflects on the travails and opportunities of education in one simple line that has very deep meanings. He says that education is the panacea of nation states. The layman would say that the ambition that drives most people to pursue education is the assurance of life chances.

Critics might have contrary views. Education does not necessarily answer all the questions in life, which is why it is not the panacea. Rather, it is simply one of the enablers, the motivators and drivers of life.

Put quite clearly, critics might state that education does aid and serve as an enabler to create life chances. Those who successfully acquire the necessary skills and qualification are more often than not guaranteed a prosperous future for themselves and their families. Needless to emphasize though, that success comes at a price.

Reflecting on what might have driven them to pioneer this educational project, which we call IAMTECH today, Paula explains meaningfully.

"Since the end of the civil war in Sierra Leone there have been immensely significant paradigm shifts. These shifts are found in the perceptions of society about the pursuit of education. Despite all the destructions that the war brought to bear on the nation, there has been a massive growth in the number of intakes in schools and the tertiary sector. In contrast to the pre war years, it is amazing that the overall surge in the numbers of the completion rates in schools, colleges and universities has not been even, let alone colossal"

"This shift has also become associated with the demands of the complex and fluid nature of the modern job markets of our day and age. For instance, the challenges associated with securing a decent job are more often than not a harrowing experience for most people, except those with the relevant skills qualifications and experiences"

Her husband, Professor Dr Paul Kamara adds: "I must emphasize the importance of acquiring the skills and qualification which are capable of meeting the challenges of the twenty-first-century world of science and technology. Abie, my wife is right. These realities have led to the demand for diversification in the tertiary sector. The few universities under the umbrella of the University of Sierra Leone are not adequate for the growing demands of the number of students desperate to acquire the necessary skills and qualifications so that they may earn decent jobs. In brief the numbers of those aspiring to acquire university degrees have outstripped the number of tertiary educational institutions in post war Sierra Leone. We need more universities in post war Sierra Leone"

These two pioneers and partners are visionaries in their own rights. They have struck the correct notes, which make their comments more informative and educative. They are ideal for a vital policy rethink in the country's new bid to revitalize standards and equal opportunities in education.

Little wonder the couple decided to establish the model of tertiary education that is one of the few tertiary institutions that capitalizes on inculcating modern skills that meet the requirements and demands of modern job markets. Little wonder that they consistently argue that the country needs more universities and that IAMTECH is a fitting candidate for this enviable status in the world of academia.

These key points mentioned above have inspired the ongoing rapid diversification in the sector, which should be treated with all the seriousness it deserves. They have inspired the climate for a healthy debate and competition beyond the walls of the Ministry of Education Science and Technology (MEST) and academia. They have reignited the ambitions of well meaning Sierra Leoneans to join the coalition for the rapid and continuing establishment of private colleges, especially in the metropolitan areas.

It has come as no surprise that post-war Sierra Leone boasts many private colleges and training outfits, in addition to the many branches of the old higher teacher training colleges such as Milton Margai College of Education through upgrading, Freetown Teachers College, Bo Teachers College and a host of others, including Polytechnics.

The rapid ratification of a bill in Parliament in this regard as well as other accreditation cases counts as instructive references. Recently a bill was ratified in Parliament giving the green light for the establishment of the Ernest Bai Koroma University of Science and Technology. The accreditation of the University of Makeni in the last couple of years buttresses the inferences further. Put together, they are all living testimonies of the calls, the movement for the surge in the numbers of universities in the country.

However I would argue that this intensive strategy or aspiration which some theorists of comparative education refer to as arithmetical or massive increases in student numbers has not necessarily solved the inherent problems of the education system. What will be fundamental is massive investment and logistical support. As I have said repeatedly, successful governments have dedicated money to support education. However, massive financial support and the quests for appropriate courses, discipline and professionalism remain the lingering problems.

The signs are glaring that there have been substantial deficits in the fundamental requirements I have mentioned. The deficits include relevant courses and programmes and lagging standards in our schools, colleges and universities. These deficits have given rise to another set of problems. Together, these problems have blurred the significance and real impact of education in the country.

Critics argue that because the impacts of education are not felt in real terms (functional outcomes), for example in the economy and other related institutions of state and national development, it must conclude that the polity has made no significant difference and so the problems linger. The enduring deficits can be replenished if you like the vacuums can be filled by financing education sensibly with accountability, fairness and equity at the heart of an urgently revamped government policy.

I must emphasize that neither the problems nor reachable solutions to them are lost on the minds of the government. This assertion is sustained by the Eleven Point of President Koroma, quoted earlier in this book. Among other things, they allude to the massive financial investments the nation requires in order to create and sustain relevance and quality in the country's education.

In hind-sight, the actual and ideal strategy that the nation's social planners should have embarked on in the immediate post war years was to ensure that the increase in schools and colleges match the viability of the required courses, skills and qualifications in relation to the new, technologically sophisticated demands of the job market. These are the key elements that are required at the tertiary level. They form the kernels of the reforms which government has contemplated in this post war time. They could turn out to be the answer to the enduring problems.

Stakeholders should not lose sight of other salient requirements. They are the adoption of appropriate disciplines, skills in modern technology and creative and critical thinking skills. Let us make no mistake in the twenty-first century these skills are in high demand. Again these salient points are implied in the President's Eleven Points for skills and quality renewal in these difficult times. That should be the case because the job markets have posed the difficult questions that the tertiary sector in post war Sierra Leone has yet to fully answer with tangible convictions and substantial results.

Again the question arises, how did these past flaws in the system impact on the thinking of the pioneers of IAMTECH? It is fair to state that Paul and Paula were quick to recognize that critical questions were being asked of the operation, management and functions of the sector, particularly the tertiary tier. They moulded their institution alongside the prerequisites of success, which should be premised on relevance and quality.

The pioneers sprang into action ambitiously, recognizing this very exciting phenomenon. They tuned teaching and staff management with these critical issues firmly in mind. And it has to be said that since the inception of the college, it has dealt with these generic problems successfully. It is gratifying to note that most private providers in the tertiary sector are now aspiring to work harder in order to catch up with the IAMTECH model of education.

By virtue of their hard work and innovation as private sector providers the proprietors and founders of IAMTCEH have earned an honourable place in the minds and imaginations of society. Most of their compatriots honour them as humanitarians and philanthropists. And rightly so judging by their contributions to country and humanity they do genuinely deserve the accolades their compatriots have accorded them. Their contributions to humanity and country will be dealt with comprehensively in a separate chapter.

The motto of IAMTECH is "For Country and For Humanity" It espouses a profound philosophy that calls for and practices sacrifice in the name of country and humanity. For the past twenty five years, this philosophy has resonated through the deeds, ideas, ideals and beliefs of the students and the entire administrative team.

Hence, it is an understatement to state that Paul and Paula are mere pioneers. The enormous successes they have achieved in pioneering the private model of tertiary education in Sierra Leone surpasses the contributions often made by mere pioneers.

# 12

# Sweat and Blood

The success stories of Paul and Paula didn't come on the cheap. They didn't have it handed over on a silver platter. It was not privileged origins as with some people. Instead the couple worked extremely hard against all the odds, in order to achieve their dream. The reason is simple because on the journey to success, no matter how smooth it might be, once in a while, there are hiccups, challenges along the route.

These challenges constitute part and parcel of most of the real stories of successful people. Ask most successful people how they achieved their success. They must have gone through difficulties of tremendous proportion. So the pioneers of this amazing story are no different when it comes to these realities. They encountered certain problems during their two- and-half decade journey.

History has it that three main factors are responsible for the success of most pioneers or any one engaged in endeavours that involve hard work and determination. They are sincerity, trust, and faith. These three virtues are invaluable in the general narratives and analyses of the success stories of these two pioneers and remarkable partners.

It is in these three virtues that they have found the magical chemistry that has cemented the bond between them from the genesis of their journey to this day, in search of success. Most significant of all, the virtues are at the heart of the amazing story of this national project under discussion. It is the interaction of these three virtues that has impacted immensely on "country and humanity"

Good begets good, the saying goes. In case one is prompted to ask about the backgrounds and origins of Mr and Mrs Kamara, it is not difficult to claim that the orientations of their origins truly match their general contributions to national development. First we begin with Dr Mrs Abie Paula Kamara. The blood of royalty runs through the veins of this patriotic, hardworking, devoted, loyal wife and pioneer. So also in their children!

In African customs and traditions, royalty is inherited. The African hereditary rights are the prototypes, if not entirely similar, to the ones ascribed to the British monarchy in the United Kingdom. According to African traditions and customs which govern the institutions of Paramount Chieftaincy, after the death of her grandfather, Paula's father inherited the rights of succession and was crowned Paramount Chief.

The rights to inherent power are ascribed to a Ruling House. Their Ruling House is called the Bai Maro Lamina Ruling House. It is in the Loko Masama Chiefdom, Port Loko District, in the Northern Province of Sierra Leone. The period in which her grandfather reigned was when men were easily separated from the boys. It was a period or an era when the institution of Paramount Chieftaincy was held in awe by subjects. They virtually ruled over the freedom and rights of their subjects.

Paramount Chiefs decided which parcel of lands and landed properties went to the subjects or households of their royal seal and choice. I am not in any measure suggesting that the institution was autocratic or despotic. This piece of description or characterization goes a long way to emphasize the power and authority of the divine rights of the institution of Paramount Chieftaincy.

Unlike the institution of the British monarchy, in most of Africa, including Sierra Leone, the institution of Paramount Chieftaincy is either patriarchal or matriarchal. In Paula's paternal home, the right to the throne is patriarchal, meaning the inheritors are males not females. Also, Paramount Chiefs are traditional rulers with supernatural gifts and powers. They are gifted with mystical powers and authority, among other myths.

Hence holders of this all-powerful position don't die a natural death they simply join their ancestors and then the battles for succession come to the fore. Another major difference between the British and African royal institutions is unique. As regards the latter, many pretenders put forward their claims to ascend the throne the moment the Paramount Chief joins his or her ancestors.

There have been enormous paradigm shifts in the modern institution of Paramount Chieftaincy. There are defined rules which govern succession, especially now that modernity has influenced the running of the institution of traditional rulers, including Paramount Chieftaincy. It involves bitter battles, to the extent that impostors even try their luck. That departs from the customs and traditions and the dicta of the gods during the reign of Paula's grandfather.

When their father PC Bai Sama Kamara joined his ancestors, he was succeeded by Paula's junior brother, the current Paramount Chief. But one has to state that it involved a herculean task before he won the battle and sat on the present royal throne of their forefathers.

The symbol of royalty is referred to as the staff in the customary history of Paramount Chieftaincy in Sierra Leone. Unlike her paternal side, on Paula's maternal side, the females are allowed to become Paramount Chiefs. Her mother is also a royalty hailing from the Alimamy Lahai Ruling House. It is in the Kawula Township in the Masumgbala Chiefdom, in the Kambia District. The Ruling House is called Alimamy Lahai Ruling House.

Luck would fall far short of describing the miracle that has been showered on the couples and their children. Each of them has become a beneficiary of the benevolent qualities of Paul and Paula. The couples have showered these children with unbounded love, care and tenderness. They have nurtured and carved a brilliant future for them. The ball is now in their court it is their responsibility to work hard, zealously seek the future carved out for them and gain the most out of it.

The amazing success story of the partnership between Paul and Paula had a humble beginning. When they both ventured out in search of knowledge and greener pastures in 1988, they landed in the United Kingdom. As expected it was not an easy adventure, although a prevailing perception of the United Kingdom paints rosy pictures for migrants. Most people think that in the United Kingdom, dreams are easily fulfilled without breaking a sweat.

Those who have ventured out in search of greener pastures know too well that this perception is at best a myth. When one considers the ratio of those who have failed to achieve success as opposed to the few lucky ones who have made it abroad, this lofty rosy perception must be dismissed as a mirage of the gold-paved streets of Europe and America and elsewhere.

Historically, the perception is a myth because all successful nations on earth have struggled throughout the period of their development. Generally speaking, considering how competitive the world has become, it is a continuous struggle to achieve success. Are people in tune with this reality at all? Arguably they are not.

Despite this undisputed fact of life, a growing generation of day-dreamers believe wholeheartedly that the streets of London are paved with diamonds and gold. Therefore in their opinion, all immigrants are assured of becoming mega rich overnight.

On the contrary, Paul and Paula were not that ambivalent. They broke sweat after sweat in order to attain their goals which equipped and inspired them to return home and become the successful pioneers they are today. They are realists and have faith in the Creator, so in the face of the difficulties they encountered on their journey, they looked to the future.

# 13

# The Big Dream

It is the natural character of people that they are made to dream or at least live that way. Otherwise, life itself becomes fruitless. And empty livelihood is utterly useless for humans and their surroundings. However, dreams which are not actualized or realized to fruitful effects remain nothing but futile dreams.

Based on the overall outputs of IAMTECH over the more than two decades now, there is no doubt that Paul and Paula are more than mere dreamers. They are concrete dreamers whose actions are planned properly and executed perfectly. Both at the time they were abroad and when they returned home, this perception about them has been true and is sustained.

When they started the project in 1991, little did most Sierra Leoneans realize that their dream project would become a reality from whose fruits everyone would gain. This points up what realists they truly are. Their realism is arched systematically along each step of the way, on the journey in search for success with the sensitivity it deserves.

One realist once said to a team of social planners as follows: "We live a very complex, changing world, so sensitivity is extremely necessary in all actions and decisions we take"

The Kamaras put their realism to work the moment they entered the United Kingdom. Unlike other migrants, they held different views regarding the challenges migrants face in England and elsewhere in Europe and in the United States. They did not harbour unrealistic expectations and quick fixes and results. They were aware of their limitations, so they didn't set bars too high for them to reach.

Migration is a critical, social, and even sometimes a political problem. Therefore we have to be realistic here. Migration from one country to another has its inherent risks and disadvantages. Even those who migrate abroad on scholarships are bound to come across obstacles.

Look at it from this view. Citizens in their own countries often suffer from hardship, let alone those who migrate to foreign countries. Migration entails enormous problems which are not for the faint-hearted. These obstacles include how to deal with the daily challenges of cultural shocks to which immigrants are subjected. Especially, these shocks are often heightened for immigrants with ambitious hearts and dispositions.

I would also caution that migration is not always naturally a terrible risk-taking venture after all life itself is a risk. There are immigrants that attain their goals abroad without breaking a sweat. Because life in general is a risky business, all humans and their endeavours are at risk. Don't we often hear stories of untimely death in the confine of the victims' comfortable homes? Surely we do. Others die whilst drinking a cup of tea or sipping a soft drink. These truisms are some of the indisputable facts of life.

The Kamaras have a remarkable trademark which defines their characters and interpersonal relationships. And it has to be said that they apply them to those around them and by extension to society at large. It is an enviable quality that has elevated them to the heights they enjoy today in society.

As philanthropists, they are always ready to help and they are not bullish about it rather they give humbly and freely to those in need. There are concrete signs of their philanthropy in the communities they serve.

Success has its inherent ambition, challenges and sometimes permanent hazards. The Kamaras are extremely ambitious. It is that which took them to England in the first place. But as the saying goes, ambition, like success comes with a price. Hence it comes as no surprise that the couples had their fair shares of the opportunities as well as difficulties most immigrants encounter abroad.

However, they proved time and again that they were up to the arduous challenges and tasks. They overcame the challenges and obstacles put in their way and maximized to the fullest the opportunities that England provides for sober, ambitious and determined minds. That being said, luck or what you might call destiny did play a major role in the successes they had in England.

I cannot overstate that their homecoming was also informed by patriotism. The patriotism of the couples is remarkable. Whilst others stay abroad after their studies and enjoy greener pastures, for them it was time to head for home. They decided to pack, return to their beloved country, Sierra Leone and give a helping hand to its socioeconomic development. One can only reach the conclusion that their dreams have come true because their patriotism has borne immense fruit for themselves and their beloved country.

I have returned to the issue of success and destiny as significant signifiers of their dream project and its fruition. They say one needs a bit of luck in order to marshal success in life. For example it is luck or destiny when we find ourselves in the right places at the right times. But we must emphasize the crucial importance of efforts, no matter how modicum it is. When you find yourself in the right place at the right time and gain success, you have to make use of your gains.

The success story of the Kamara family is no exception. On balance, one can say that although they are blessed with immense luck, they blended the strengths of hard work and the determination to succeed. They are grateful to their Creator that they had the better of both worlds.

Reflecting on the most important decision they had to take, Paula laments: "We'd spent close to thirty years in England. Yes, it is a land of opportunity and we held our own there against all the odds. But it came to a time when nostalgia and other natural, patriotic feelings and sentiments had the better of our homecoming emotions and desires. It was then that we realized that it was time for us to return home and serve our people and country"

"The decision was inspired significantly by our burning desires to serve our country and humanity. By the time we'd spent a decade in England, we fully became aware of the fact that there is sense in the decision of the Creole breed in Sierra Leone". I was curious when she mentioned the attitudes of the Creole when they venture abroad, so I asked her. "What is the point you are making about the Creole breed abroad?"

"The Sierra Leonean Creole migrants abroad always return home to Sierra Leone, from wherever they may be in order to serve. The first generation of Creoles that migrated overseas returned home the moment they acquired their necessary qualifications because they believe in the adage that there is no place like home"

Paul added: "We received mountains of pressure from our families and good friends in our homeland to return home. My wife and I had acquired the necessary skills and qualifications. We also backed them up with rich experiences in the English job markets. In the end, we believed that we could profitably utilize these treasures in our homeland, Sierra Leone. I always admonished my wife that if we were to return home, we should make a huge difference"

"Why?" I asked.

Paul: "Make a huge difference by becoming assets to our country and humanity not as liabilities"

By virtue of the profiles of husband and wife, they were well equipped and also capable of making worthy contributions to national development. Paul is an engineer by trade and had had massive practical and managerial experiences in a reputable mining corporation established in Sierra Leone.

As an added advantage, Paul has an intuitive business acumen, backed by strong technical skills. Those skills are strongly rooted in his engineering background. Four decades ago, he wrote a comprehensive booklet on a critical aspect of engineering as a student. He made this booklet available to me recently when I started this writing project.

I must confess that with my instinctive phobia, coupled with teenage dismay for anything that has to do with figures or technical disciplines, such as the one he has mastered, I was fascinated by the sophistication of the booklet's contents. My verdict is that it is an extremely rich booklet. The technical drawings, the physics and the allied scientific theories with practical interpretations all form the rich narratives of the booklet, making it most instructive.

When I read the booklet, I was thrilled, so I asked him. "What do you want us to do, turn it into a future book?"

He released an unassuming smile and answered, "In the near future, we might develop the booklet into a book. "Then he asked, "What do you think?"

"I believe that this booklet could be developed into an educative textbook for engineering students and lecturers"

During their years as migrants in England, Paul added more feathers to his cap. He undertook numerous courses as well as amassing fertile experiences in various modern software packages. Those were the days when these forms of technology were not fully in vogue in most educational institutions in Sierra Leone.

Not only were basic computing courses, tutors and experts extremely, scarce commodities. Sierra Leone was not a peculiar case. Even England and other parts of the capitalist Western world suffered from the scarcity of these vital innovations which have gripped the modern world of technology.

Although the first computer was actually manufactured in England (its mediocrity notwithstanding) during what was in effect the Dark Ages it was popularized in the United States of America and elsewhere in the advanced world. Britain fell in love with the theoretically oriented skills and so, the service and hospitality industries have overtaken technology.

In most of Africa, literacy in computer and information technology was on the verge of inspiring new realization, especially in educational institutions. Its relevance surpassed most disciplines, to the extent that it became compulsory the touchstone for any curriculum to be deemed as viable. The popularity and necessity of skills and knowledge in information technology profoundly marked the onset of a new awareness in the continent.

However, considering the socioeconomic constraints, compounded by less enthusiastic political climate and bureaucratic tendencies, only a fortune few actually had the opportunity to see and work with computers by the close of the twentieth century. Amazingly this reality persists even age fifteen years on.

Therefore one could say that it was destiny that the couples decided to concentrate on the acquisition of this brand of knowledge and skills.

Little did they themselves realize at the time, that skills in information technology would be the profound leverage that would propel them to distinction in their future endeavours in Sierra Leone!

As stated Paul has the knack for technology and all engineering related techniques. He manifested these gifts in England and China. For instance, in the People's Republic of China, he invented new techniques in the manufacturing of pumps and water engineering technology. The invention was validated, and he was dully rewarded by the Chinese. To this day, he receives annual royalties in the form of reasonable sums of money for this great piece of engineering.

Some months ago he gave me another shocker. It was a comprehensive compilation he completed years ago whilst in school. "I don't know, but I think we could publish this in the near future. Won't we?" he asked with a broad smile.

The book is a massive and detailed text in engineering with intricate, sophisticated technical drawing diagrams backed by theories which could easily intimidate those with phobias about the pure and applied sciences or anything that has to do with technology. It is this literature of his that has educated me about the man's skills and acumen in a discipline that he enjoys and holds dear to his heart because he is good at it. No wonder China has faith in his engineering ability!

Like her husband, Paula also equipped herself with the necessary skills and qualifications. She studied information and computer technology. But prior to that, she had acquired her teaching certificate at the Port Loko Teacher Training College in the Northern Province of Sierra Leone. To acquire practical professional experience, she taught successfully in schools in Sierra Leone for years before the couples migrated to the United Kingdom.

After completing a number of advanced courses in information technology and systems, she acquired higher qualifications in educational administration. Paula surely followed in the steps of her husband, who added educational administration to his massive collections in engineering and information systems.

Together, the couples mustered their wealth of qualifications and the skills they acquired. They were conscious that these are the very veritable gems, the assets from which their compatriots and the rest of society would one day benefit immensely.

Paul and Paula think and plan alike, which has been one of the secrets of their glittering success stories. But one can state that fate is always on their side, to the extent that they were surely destined to become husband and wife. They were also destined for great achievements. They are gratified that their dream project has made a huge difference in the lives of their compatriots as the true model, the ideal education that the new Sierra Leone deserves.

# 14

# Perseverance

One religious leader and philosopher once said that it is neither by intelligence nor wealth that mankind negotiates the curves of life successfully but by divine grace. How right he was!

Beside, this word of wisdom has been made evident in the lives of the proprietors and founders of IAMTECH. Reflecting on their success stories, Paula commented with immense pride and gratitude to her Good Lord and Maker as follows:

"Since we returned home, we have paid our dues as bona fide Sierra Leoneans. This project, IAMTECH epitomizes the vision behind our homecoming. We have established it across the length and breadth of the country. It goes a long way to suggest that where there is a will, there is always a way. Above all I must say by way of homage and thanks to the Creator by declaring that to the Almighty be the glory!"

IAMTECH is a benevolent higher educational project that was founded just at the commencement of the brutal civil war in 1991. Against all odds, it has grown into one of the most popular, vibrant and successful, tertiary educational institutions in Sierra Leone.

Despite the success stories in which they are basking currently, like every human being, the couples had misgivings in their early years. They are not shy to confess that they faced challenges along their historic journey to the success they now enjoy.

Reflecting on how they survived the huddles, one can only say that they are capable of adapting and adjusting to unforeseen contingencies. It is undoubtedly the case because there is a big difference between returning home especially after spending many years abroad, learn and adopting new cultures and ways of doing things and behaving unpretentiously.

We should not also forget that in Africa, running any project entails negotiating considerable political difficulties. Therefore the demands of their journey also required endurance and the ability to cope with the complex political, social and economic challenges on the ground.

Life in Africa is quite different from life in Europe. Apart from that, the reality is that resettlement in a new terrain entails herculean tasks for anyone.

As the day-to-day manager of the home, Paula was eager to comment on the vital social issues they had to deal with:

"My husband and I were not necessarily afraid nor were we timid to return to our homeland after our studies in England. The only doubts that kept lingering in our minds and tormenting us had to do specifically with the fear of failure. Of course, England is a difficult place to live, work and study at the same time especially during our own time it was not easy by any stretch of the imagination"

She threw light on the policies and politics in the UK at the time under discussion.

"The Conservatives were in power and the immigration laws were tough. Immigrants had to hustle in order to secure jobs, and Britain was in the middle of a nail-biting economic recession. There were few jobs for which indigenes and immigrants had to compete. For ambitious migrants, like us, combining work and the acquisition of education compounded our problems"

This should not be interpreted as trying to paint the picture of an enthusiastic feminist or gender advocate. To my mind, when it comes to attaining the second highest political office in Britain, which is the post of premiership, the chances for females are very slim, although the Head of State, the Queen of Great Britain and the Commonwealth is a female.

Yes, female politicians do attain ministerial, cabinet positions, even at that the ratio is not in their favour Britain, as also their former colonies is a male dominated society. Since records began, the only female that has ever become Prime Minister in Great Britain is the one popularly and affectionately known as the Iron Lady. Mrs Margaret Thatcher. Mrs Thatcher was a formidable leader and personality.

Her critics referred to her as a divisive political figure. Maybe the criticisms were due to the fact that she was a no-nonsense person. Mrs Thatcher stood by whatever she said and did at the time.

Amazingly even though the challenges brought to bear on the immigrant community in Britain were meant to militate against their chances of success, Paul and Paula did pull through.

Paula continued, "My husband I worked our socks off, and eventually we decided to return home to our fatherland and embark on the project that is meant to increase opportunities for our brothers and sisters. It was our ultimate goal. So any thought of unforeseen impediments or failures was a dreadful proposition, let alone should that becomes a possibility"

Paul recounted his own reflections regarding the fate of their children once they returned to Sierra Leone:

"As my wife has said rightly, we didn't want to come home and fail but we were determined to return home come what may. Our patriotic instincts convinced us that this is our home and that there is no place as worthy as home for us in Sierra Leone. But like all parents the needs and considerations of our children were paramount to us"

"We had settled abroad for close to three decades with our children. In England, they felt very much at home because they could get things done with ease in seconds. What I mean is that in England schooling is well organized and so they were very comfortable, unlike in Africa where things are not that straightforward. Our children had also made their childhood and teenage friends abroad. They wouldn't dream of being left behind in England"

"Some of the public services considered as routine endeavours in England and elsewhere in the advanced world are milestones that are not readily reachable and available in most of Africa. Basic routines such as transportation to get to school and back are affordable abroad easily. There was also the issue of not readily available teaching and learning resources.

The quality of the physical school environment and the general ethos of the very teachers that would teach our children were concerns we had to consider seriously. Don't get us wrong, considering the circumstances, Sierra Leone was doing relatively well"

The state and quality of education in the country was the most serious factor the family had to worry about. Sierra Leone prides itself on quality education and the history of the country confirms this thesis. It is known as the Athens of West Africa and home to the first seat of higher learning dating from 1827, as pointed out already.

But like most African countries, Sierra Leone has gone through decades of political, social and economic challenges since political independence in 1961. These years of compounded problems have been dubbed the trying era or the lost decades of Sierra Leone.

It was as if the departure of the British colonialists symbolized the departure or death of progress in the successful socioeconomic spheres of the country. Paradoxically, the African literary critics would have an opposite view. They counter that the very colonial masters were partly responsible for the depravity and degradation of most of Africa, including Sierra Leone. Hence their departure didn't mark the death and obituary of socioeconomic progress instead they left the vices behind as the very track records of their colourful colonial legacies, which could be counted in failures.

The above misgivings and doubts nearly plagued the minds of the Kamara family. They nearly shattered their hopes and decision to return home.

Echoing my views, Paula commented "We nearly gave up and stayed put in England"

To add insult to injury, unfortunately, their doubts and misgivings about returning home were sustained by some of the very misgiving and phobias of some of their Sierra Leonean friends abroad. Some of these Sierra Leoneans had spent decades abroad and had few intention of returning home.

There might be many explanations and arguments for their phobias. The popular explanation is that the "homecoming doom mongers" had failed abroad and had nothing to offer back home. Hence, there was a fear on the part of the anti home returnees that they would be ridiculed on their arrival, especially if they returned empty handed.

Let us give these so-called "homecoming doom mongers" the credit they deserve. Some of them hadn't necessarily contributed to the reasons for their mishaps or failings. They were not their own nemesis. Those who were had no skills and qualifications, not even a penny to invest or support themselves and their loved ones they had abandoned for ages in Sierra Leone.

Paul commented on the fears of their fellow Sierra Leoneans who advised them against their homecoming dream but admonished them to stay and relish the "good life" in England.

"One of my own very bosom friends advised us not to leave the luxuries and opportunities in England and return to Sierra Leone. I remember, he asked me at one time, 'How can you abandon certainty for uncertainty?'"

Let us look squarely at the bigger picture and approach the argument regarding the "homecoming "doom mongers" I am not at all arguing in favour of the homecoming doubters and those who harbour such phobias, but most Sierra Leone nationals who went abroad like the Kamaras did hardly dreamt of returning to Sierra Leone. The reasons were glaring. Two or so decades into the post-independence era, some appalling conditions painted a grotesque picture of dilapidation in almost all facets of our national institutions.

Two foreign journalists captured the political and socioeconomic moods of the period we are talking about.

The first BBC reporter said: "The economic meltdown in Sierra Leone at that time affected the weight of the national currency, the Leone. It depreciated considerably. The prospect of economic recovery was hardly a realistic forecast by any Nobel winning economist. Not even for the foreseeable future"

The second BBC reporter recalled. "All was doomed. On top of that was the nation killer disease that hindered all strides towards national development. The viruses of the disease were found in the misappropriation of public funds, lack of transparency, accountability, and the enduring divisive nepotism and tribalism that inhibited the general progress of the nation. Together, these problems formed the basis of the political and social unrests of the time. They were the inherent causes of the national political instability of the late 1980s and with the passage of time they cemented the factors that led to the devastating civil war in 1991"

It was a period whose mayhem was also captured by political commentators and analysts at home in Sierra Leone. This coming forth openly was as a result of the fact that the wider ramification of the national diseases mentioned above reached a degree that people were constrained to talk about it.

Read on:

"The power grabbing craze and madness crippled the socioeconomic progress of Sierra Leone en masse. Major players and contenders of the power grabbing craze were the military brass. During that period, they hardly stayed in their barracks. Incessant coups of complex descriptions were in vogue. Significantly, it was a period of incessant military coups. There were regular, military coups and counter coups, with few successes. Sometimes mixtures of civilian and military coups were conducted by disgruntled soldiers and civilians. Other times, counter insurgencies were into the obnoxious mix"

The unsavoury socio-political climate undermined the only valuable legacies of the British colonialists. They were democratic elections, accountability and obedience to the rule of law. These values were swept aside violently. Sometimes, these coups and undemocratic machinations were lethal, deadly, resulting in curfews and summary executions.

One political analyst resident in Sierra Leone at the time described the period eloquently in the same manners as the ones just quoted. The description reads as follows:

"It was an era of madness and craze for political power and wealth. Elections were rigged freely, and with impunity. The Sierra Leone political class didn't recognize pluralistic politics in their political dictionary. Multiparty democracy was a taboo, an anathema. These vices were further compounded by bitter ethnic and regional rivalry, all for acquisition of political power and amassing wealth"

The saying goes that it is only those with faith and the right attitudes who will shine through even in the most hazardous of times. Despite all the misgivings and doubts they had, Paul and Paula returned home in 1992, when the civil war had just begun.

It was indeed a brave decision, to say the least. How could anyone in their right mind leave the safe and secure conditions in Europe with immense opportunities there for the taking? They took all the risks which were prevalent in Africa, including Sierra Leone at the time of the civil war, returned home and set up their dream project IAMTECH.

Paula concluded sagely, "It was by virtue of Divine Grace, that we had the tenacity to decide so bravely against all the odds and return home. Come what may, we were determined to try the tides and swim"

# PART FIVE

# 15

# Sweet Home

Decades ago when I was a naïve, primary pupil, I was amazed by the repeated, sayings of one of our teachers. He used to grumble: "If you want to be a millionaire go and mine diamonds, Better still become an international smuggler of our precious produces and minerals across the Liberia Sierra Leone borders. Don't choose teaching. Teachers are naturally married to chastity, which is why they can't become rich in this life. My parents and those who taught me always admonished me that riches await teachers in the next world"

---

Maybe my former teacher was right, but teacher or not, the socioeconomic landscapes and realities have changed considerably since then. The fact is that when one reflects on the general conditions of service for teachers in Sierra Leone, the miseries by which they are defined now are by no means new phenomena.

Prior to the vicious, civil war, the deplorable, national socioeconomic deteriorations had destabilized politics in society. There were cascading effects on all forms of national development. They seriously affected the day-to-day administration and financing of educational institutions and the teaching profession. There were regular class closures, due either to military coups or strikes by teachers and students over the chronic, enduring, appalling social and economic conditions. These malaises were compounded by often delayed payments of salaries and a shortage of money in the national bank.

Of course, the take-home pay package for teachers was a mere pittance.

One veteran head teacher who survived the storms at that time commented: "No sober person will call our pay packets reasonable salaries at all. The fact is that the general conditions of service for teachers were appalling"

This was the climate in which Paul and Paula had to operate. Put mildly, it was a chaotic situation where only brave pragmatists could afford to live and fend for their bread, let alone establish a project like IAMTECH. Nevertheless, the Kamara family did all in the name of patriotism and gambled.

Whether we call it nostalgia, initiative, or instinctive patriotism and nationalist fuels that ignited their homecoming passion, the Kamaras were energized to return home to sweet Sierra Leone at last. All doubts were swept aside by a surge of euphoric nostalgia to the extent that they could no longer postpone their homecoming journey.

In that fateful year they boarded the plane from London and flew in at the Lungi International Airport. They happily disembarked in the land of their ancestors. Little did they know that, that very day marked the little giant step made first, for themselves, and then for mankind. That first step heralded what was to create an everlasting impact on their lives and the lives of multitudes across the length and breadth of Sierra Leone. Like seeds, the impacts blossomed and the fruits have spread gradually to amazing effects. These gratuitous seeds have grown gracefully. They have grown against all the odds and they have made tremendous difference in the lives of many people within and beyond the shores of their cherished Sierra Leone.

I have met most of their children since we became bosom friends. Their names are Peter Aziz Kamara, Pualina Mbalu Kamara, Paul Abass Kamara Jr, Paulina Theresa Kamara, Joseph Michael Kamara and Peter Unmaru Kamara. They all speak with one voice, in family unity.

One of their children has elegant ideas like his parents. He has taken voluntary retirement from the British Armed Forces, one of the most distinguished militaries in the world. He had a distinguished career, rising to the rank of Staff Sergeant. He is currently serving as an intelligence officer for the United Nations Organization.

Paula and her husband commented with joy on the blessings of their children, when I congratulated them for being enriched with enormous blessings.

"You people are richly blessed, "I stated.

Paula commented, "Thanks to God, we are extremely proud and blessed to state that our children have inherited so many productive and virtuous qualities from us. One of these qualities is the ethics of hard work, determination to succeed and discipline"

The Kamara family and I have come a long way. It was in 2012 that I started lodging with them at their St Paul Drive residence in Freetown. At no time did I witness any manner of waywardness or indiscipline among the children. They are always either busy with their books or engaged in domestic chores. The entire building is full of the effigies of their faith. They are devout, committed and benevolent Catholics.

The children have amazing intelligence, crowned by their intellectual commitments. Miss Paulina Kamara is reading law at Fourah Bay College, University of Sierra Leone. She has all it takes to make a future diligent lawyer. In addition to her roles in the Church, she participates in extra curricular activities, such as serving in the community and undertaking literary endeavours.

One of Paulina's unique characteristics is that she comes across very much as a bookworm. This young lady can hardly pass a second without opening a legal textbook or documents or reading a rich novel of substance. This ambitious young lady made a lasting impressing on me when I took my first romantic novel, called "*Virgin Island*", to Freetown. I gave the book to her mother as a present, but she took it away and got hooked on it, and in less time than expected, this bookworm had read the fat novel to the end.

These are amazing characteristics one can hardly find in most of our young people these days. I say this with assurance, because we are in a time of waywardness amongst young people. There are what we call misplaced priorities amongst the youth. Most of them are tied to either the internet, mobile phones, pads, or other wayward social endeavours instead of books, and intellectual activities bring annoyance to their minds. The appetites of most young people are sadly on the wane. They have been overtaken by the massive magical influences of modern social media. Amazingly, Miss Paulina Kamara is quite the opposite.

Generically speaking, social waywardness has become an erratic virus. It could be said of even some members of the adult world. Unfortunately instead of playing the role of instructors and good role models, some have twisted minds these days.

There is hardly any time set aside on the calendars of most adults for the preservation of law and order, moral rectitude or emulating good character and behaviour or engaging in grand intellectual endeavours. Pleasurable activities have profound impacts on the minds of people these days. Creativity has been killed deliberately. Anything that has to do with creativity or intellectual exercise is boring and all is vanity!

Young Paula's behaviour is efficacious and the manner in which she carries herself very much suits the dignified and learned culture, norms and values of the legal profession. She has aspired to pursue a career for which she is well suited.

This young lady has emulated the distinguished conduct of her parents with ease. I say so because teenagers her age typically throw caution to the wind and move with the times. Miss Paulina Kamara is different teenager. She is carbon copy of Mrs Abie Paula Kamara, her dignified mother in every sense.

IAMTECH is the pride of the children. They are very much aware that their parents have created a legacy for which all of them will be honoured. Its Silver Jubilee as a tertiary college will be celebrated in the early months of 2016. The college may be new but has achieved much success. It has planted magnificent seeds of enormous progress and these seeds have become national assets.

The success stories of the concrete seeds this institution has grown in these past two decades are benefits worth emulating. They have made a historic impact and become beneficial to multitudes in post war Sierra Leone.

One benefit that the pioneering endeavours of Paul and Paula have brought to the new Sierra Leone is to give new meanings to the tertiary provision in the education sector. The well-tailored curriculum contents of their programmes underscore the new meanings of the ideal type of tertiary education.

The message is clear and simple programmes or courses are not independent of the requirements of job markets as well as the communities served by institutions. Therefore, they must be tailored to the strict requirements of the factories, industries, shops, police and armed forces and of civil service offices. They must be tailored to suit the requirements of the teaching profession.

I must clarify the point that the new meanings are not meant to undermine the intrinsic values or the inner satisfaction of education per se. The new message this philosophy emphasizes is clear and simple. Especially in the tertiary sector, the emphasis is to combine theoretical and practical vocational skills.

It is not ideal or feasible anymore to just stress the intrinsic values of education. What about the skills that contribute to socioeconomic development? The realities are correlative and equally important in order to bring beauty, success and happiness to the soul. They are critical for the short as well as long-term success of educational programmes.

We must also remember that certain social and political cultures are hazardous. Like epidemic viruses they hinder the values of education. In most of Africa, the vices of tribalism or negative ethnicity have put a knife on the values and unity that normally bind the nation together.

In the Sierra Leone situation, sometimes the vices of tribalism and regional affiliation are made to afflict people through the remote controls of the predatory techniques of the flies. These tsetse flies are some politicians who bite in a subtle but effective manner to deadly effect. Hence, for success in business enterprises including education, agents must be colour blind. They must depart from these vices if they would like to clock success.

Personal attributes of IAMTECH's stakeholders, including founders and proprietors count as well. To the credit of the proprietors and founders of IAMTECH, they dispense the qualities that breed success. They are colour blind and diligent in their endeavours. They work with people regardless of differences in race, nationality, region, gender, religion or socioeconomic status. In their comprehensive testimonies and tributes to them, members of staff revealed that it is through these qualities that they have cemented their success stories.

# 16

# The Civil War

Skills and qualifications were in high demand during the 1991 civil war although it was the most difficult period in the history of Sierra Leone. The reason for this demand is simple the civil war drew the attention of the authorities to the salient fact that education is the answer to the lingering socioeconomic problems in the country.

Personally, this period was also critical for the couples. The calamities, which culminated into many deaths and malicious, random destructions of property, put their faith and character to the utmost test.

Paula reflected on that sad deadly, time. "We survived through faith in God. Of course we would have been dead by now, but it was by a leap of faith that we are still alive"

The IAMTECH project withstood the storms that brought education and other national institutions to a virtual standstill. The causes of the civil war have been well documented, so there is no need for us to rehearse them here. The impact it had on the architects and their project and the manner in which they pulled through are the key themes of this chapter.

The human costs of all warfare are debilitating. The scars of warfare they say, last forever. The family cannot state the specific estimates of the horrendous experiences they suffered. The loss of the lives of their loved ones and the financial costs are not quantifiable.

Stating the obvious in tears, Paula asked me a rhetorical question during the course of our interview. "Can anyone estimate the psychological traumas that are caused by warfare?"

Of course, no one can estimate the impact of traumas of any kind, let alone the debilitating warfare the nation went through for almost thirteen traumatic years. The victims of the two World Wars are still suffering from the impact of those wars to say nothing of the Sierra Leone conflict that by comparison took place yesterday.

The only consolation is that while some people in a given population can't endure traumas, others do. Those who do are the lucky ones, those referred to as the hard core. Through faith alone do they survive, because it takes more than ordinary human strength to endure the posttraumatic effects of warfare.

Despite the pains survivors of the First and Second World Wars experienced and continue to endure to this day, some of these gallant, brave, and faithful men and women have recorded the most harrowing stories of people's cruelties to their fellow humans. Through these stories humankind has had the opportunity to reflect seriously and learn sober lessons from the tragedies warfare of any kind brings into human life. These mistakes must clearly teach that warfare should be avoided at all cost.

The impact of warfare varies. Some of those who survived the Sierra Leone civil war abandoned all that they had fought for in their lives. They were constrained to leave the country before even the Lome Peace Accord was signed in the Togolese capital, Lome.

On the other hand, there were some who stayed after the conflict that were incapacitated by its posttraumatic stress. To this day, they have not regained their usefulness but remain in a vegetative state.

As mentioned before Paul and Paula endured every manner of trauma as well as political and socioeconomic setbacks and they soldiered on until they attained their goals. That concrete outcome of their goals is the IAMTECH project.

I recorded further comments from the horses' mouths. They are indeed worth producing here word-for-word when one considers the capacity and weight of their traumas and endurances. Of course they were faced with massive mountains to climb, but climb they did, at all costs.

"The civil war years were horrifying, to say the least," said Dr Mrs Abie Paula Kamara.

"I know it is hard to reflect on the pains we go through in circumstances such as the ones we are talking about. However, please, recount some of the most traumatic moments that you and your entire family will never forget," I appealed to her.

She took a deep breath and went on. "There were countless moments as you may appreciate as a Sierra Leonean that I don't want to comment on. The one that impacted most on us was the moment when my husband was forced to flee for safety. It was in very precarious circumstances"

"How precarious ?" I asked

"It was an unbearable experience. All I would like to say is that my husband is dearly committed to his family but during that time, he was forced to flee for his dear life"

In tears I asked her, "How did you cope, taking care of the children and the rest of the family?"

"Well, they say, the Lord works in mysterious ways, his wonders to perform."

"Tell me how did the Lord work His miracles, mysteries for you and your family? Tell me in a single sentence."

"When our entire family, including our children, and I least expected, that was when the man we thought had died, killed by the rebels, resurfaced miraculously to our consternations and happiness."

Although the answer was obvious, I asked "How did you and the kids feel when you saw your husband, the father of your kids?"

She uttered with a broad smile. "Given the calamities, we leaped for joy of course. But it was joy marked by tears in our bleeding eyes and pains deep down in our hearts."

Then as if she was steering in vain, she asked me pitifully, "Does that make any sense to you?"

It is a dramatic irony that sometimes evil bears or brings good tidings. The Civil Way years marked the booming period of projects in Sierra Leone. Foreign aid poured into the country to help victims as well as get survivors and their local projects back on their feet in many ways. During that period projects emerged in all forms and shapes. It was not surprising as the same happened during and after the end of the Second World War in Europe.

At the end of the First World War, the League of Nations was formed. After the Second World War, the United Nations was founded. This organization is a community of nations that has championed the good courses often referred to as humanitarian aid around the world, in particular troubled, war torn zones.

When the war broke out in Sierra Leone, the United Nations (UN), and other non governmental organizations (NGOs), converged on the country. Their key mission was the provision of humanitarian aid to the languishing victims of war.

Their efforts were augmented by various stakeholders, including local voluntary groups and the country's civil society organizations. They all worked around the policy initiatives of the government and their international partners to give aid and respite to victims of the conflict.

When the war came to an end the overall mission of the various stakeholders was expanded. They concentrated on repairing and rebuilding the wreckages left behind by the warring factions. Most of the building projects included educational institutions and government offices. In addition to repairing damaged educational institutions, they revived and regenerated the school structures.

It was during this period that the ingenuity and visions of Paul and Paula were put to work for country and humanity. They were intent on injecting new initiatives in the tertiary sector. "My husband and I dreamed of new philosophy that is ideal for post war Sierra Leone", Paul said.

"What is that philosophy if I may ask madam?" I said

"It is simple but productive. It is an educational system that is capable of teaching marketable skills and moulding good characters that will be well-placed to serve this nation."

Her husband, Paul added in one sentence, "We were aware that it is this kind of education that is essential for post-war Sierra Leone"

Their dream project had to be the focal point of the philosophy of the couple. They must get it up and running during this very difficult period in the nation's historic post war recovery period.

Like all new businesses, the project progressed only when they made enormous sacrifice. They were housed in a one bed-room house in which they ran classes. It began as a makeshift typing school, located in the outskirts of the city of Freetown, in Kissy Dockyards.

They say the Lord rewards hard work, genuine labour. With the passage of time things began to move in favour of the founders. Gradually they captured the attentions of clients, local communities and the government.

It was not too long before the institute was recognized. Then came 1996, when the Tertiary Education Commission (TEC) gave the institution their seal of approval. The institution was allowed to operate in Sierra Leone as the first private tertiary educational institution in the country. This time was crucial, because the newly approved tertiary educational institute started to gain popularity and a degree of recognition and respect among students and the communities it served. Steadily, it became a force to reckon with because the courses it offers earn students jobs at completion.

There is another amazing paradox about warfare. No matter how horrific and devastating it is, it creates a sense of awareness among victims as well as survivors and their relatives. Sierra Leoneans have become aware that education is the solution of the many causes of the conflict.

That brings us to the need to offer the right courses in higher educational institutions. Needless to say there had been massive vacuums as far as the provision of the right courses are concerned, especially in pre war Sierra Leone. Sierra Leone had established many schools as well as a handful of tertiary institutions since the 1980s. However, there were serious shortages of the relevant programmes in skills required to equip the middle manpower workforce. The corresponding effects on national development were glaring, to the extent that they couldn't be ignored anymore. Questions were asked in high places because such crucial deficits impacted on the political leadership the technocrats and experts at the helm in the nation's education ministry.

The young generation of any nation constitutes one of the main organs of its human resources. Unfortunately, since most of them were underutilized, the jobless statistics of this vital area of the national population became alarming. And the saying goes that an idle mind is often restless and could resort to mischief.

Thus, the idleness and lack of creativity imposed on the young population due to inaction on the part of the polity had wider ramifications which were unforeseen. At its height, the rebel movement seized the opportunity and manipulated the idle and disaffected youth, and deployed them to cause the mayhems the nation underwent throughout the conflict.

Have the governments that emerged after the war learned any meaningful lessons? On balance, the lessons seem to have sunk in. The growing awareness that manifested itself in presentations of academic papers and seminars about the weaknesses in the education sector during the 2015 Week of Education are glaring examples.

This renewed sense of awareness parallels an educative era of renaissance in post war Sierra Leone. It has sent a very powerful message across the length and breadth of the nation. The message is that the time is now for action no more time-wasting! And by all indications, the institutions of the family, education and the polity have been touched by this incredibly sincere message.

# 17

# Game Changers

The social and economic problems which preceded the civil conflict were dangerous hindrances to national development and political stability. At the same time standards were in decline in most places. In education, especially the tertiary sector, a game changer was required either from the private or public sector within or beyond the country.

The assets that come from the game changer or game changers were innovation and creativity in commerce, accounting, information and the science of technology, among other vital disciplines to generate wealth and ideas. These are the imminent assets that Sierra Leoneans reckoned would effectuate positive change and maximize the needed accelerated social and economic development.

One observer put it nicely: "Sierra Leone needed creative ideas in order to turn the tide in favour of sustained peace and national social and economic progress"

These considerations and requirements for national prosperity were not lost on the founders and proprietors of IAMTECH. They were determined to bring about these needed changes and they were as ready as ever to assume that unique mantle of changer.

Commenting on these salient matters Dr Mrs Abie Paula Kamara said among other things:

"We are not only founders and proprietors of IAMTECH we are bona fide Sierra Leoneans. We did not only dream of ideas, we applied them to solve these lingering problems of the middle manpower skills shortage which has persisted in the country for ages now. The proprietors and academic staff of IAMTECH are innovative. Even before we founded the institution, we had realized that there were shortfalls in the sector, so without wasting any time, we seized the initiative. Gradually IAMTECH began to find solutions to the fundamental causes of the war. We were out of the country but we were aware of the fact that these problems had lingered for decades. The most fundamental one in the tertiary sector had ever been the massive skills shortage"

Supporting the same themes, her husband, Professor Dr Paul Kamara made his points with passion:

"The social and economic development of any nation depends on the vital contributions of its educational system. Primary of all are the appropriate skills, attitudes and character, so we designed our programmes at IAMTECH to concentrate on these vital areas"

In addition to providing the right programmes, the institution also realized that policies should empower the academic and administrative staff. The management recruited junior lecturers from among former students who had successfully completed their programmes with excellent grades. They employed them not just to teach but to become positive role models of the college. They were of impeccable characters and outstanding abilities to lecture and nurture students placed in their care.

Commenting on this important policy, Paula said among other things. "The policy is symbolic as well as political. I mean that it has strong political statement inherent in it"

"How symbolic is it?" I asked her.

"It is symbolic in the sense that the local talents employed to teach serve also as iconic figures and the finished products of the good works of the institution."

"What is the political essence Madam?"

"The political message it sends is powerful"

"Please elaborate on it"

"The message fosters that the institution is a force to reckon with. It recognizes the fact that when you empower people, you give them the opportunity to prove their mettle and they assist others to do the same"

"What more Madam?"

"Transforming students into efficient and hardworking lecturers with good attitudes and behaviours consolidates the belief in IAMTECH as a viable institution. As a bonus, lecturers who perform to their utmost are given the opportunity to pursue further, advanced academic qualifications and professional training within and outside Sierra Leone"

Some of the former successful students who have benefited from these benevolent schemes and policies were enthused to lend their views freely to the discussions. I gave them the opportunity to do so. One pointed out: "I am proud to be on the staff list of this noble institution that has made me what I am today. To me, service to this institution is an honour as well as sacred duty for me to emulate the actions and benevolence of the founders"

Another spoke emotionally: "What would have become of me and my parents after graduation had IAMTECH not given me this awesome opportunity? At first, I was offered a partial scholarship which enabled me to complete my degree course. I was given another opportunity to do my master's degree at the Njala University. Now I have been further honoured to lecture at the very institution where I was once a student. This is awesome!"

I questioned this former student to comment on a salient point: "Are the offers by the Kamara family not merely gratuitous?"

He retorted: "Should I understand the gestures of the proprietors as borne out of mere sympathy?"

I clarified the point: "I mean whether you deserve the awards of both partial scholarship and job?"

"No, I think you are misinterpreting the whole thing. I was not given scholarship and job out of sympathy. I earned what I have achieved but that does not diminish the fact that they are extremely kind people"

"Do you appreciate them?"

"Undoubtedly, I am grateful to the Paul Kamara family for offering me this opportunity to prove my mettle. My God will surely bless them immensely"

Mrs Kamara was enthusiastic to stress these vital points: "They say the sweetness of the pudding is in the eating"

"What do you mean by that proverb?"I asked.

"By virtue of the performances of our former students in the job market, IAMTECH has indeed proved its mettle as one of the viable tertiary institutions in the country"

I wanted the views of the proprietor on the downside of recruiting their former students other than external applicants for jobs.

"What do you say about the policy of grooming your local talents most of the time?"

"The policy of employing our former outstanding students to lecture after graduation represents one of the core values of IAMTECH. But coming to your question, I beg to differ, because we do not only encourage external applicants, we have a good number on our staff. Generally, we target excellent, professional, committed people to lecture at IAMTECH"

One of the Heads of Departments also spoke up in honour of the policy as follows: "Through this policy we have proved to the outside world that our institution is a quality institution. This has been proved beyond all reasonable doubts. In every facet of Sierra Leone's public and private institution job market, the excellent contributions and performances of our former students are felt and recognized"

The rationale of this policy is that although the institution recruits external candidates, they emphasize or give priority to internal candidates so as to inspire and motivate those who study at IAMTECH to work hard. This policy is not peculiar to IAMTECH or even her sister institutions in the country. Institutions in Britain, America and elsewhere in the world practice the same policy among other things. It is as worthy a policy as the institution that practices it.

# 18

# Challenges

All ventures in life have their inherent challenges. Hence they say there is no success story without its obstacles. In other words, the route that leads to success is not always smooth. The monumental challenges that were put in the way of the Kamaras culminated during their trying years. Of course paramount of them all was the civil war. But for the interventions of the Creator, they would have given up when they encountered their premier huddles.

Similarly, a massive project such as the educational institution the couple dreamed of entailed mountains of problems not resolved so easily. For some in authority, the mere thought of establishing a private tertiary institution alongside the existing elitist ones is anathema. It upsets or even demeans traditional values. The matter of financing, either personal capital or statutory funding was a heavy burden.

These problems are even more acute and problematic in African countries. We all do appreciate that capital is the linchpin which can guarantee either the failure or the survival and effective administration of private institutions in African countries. Logical issues have crippled many educational projects including premises and transportation.

And then there is the human aspect, which deals with the mindsets or the psychology of the people and communities. In an African climate where private ventures are viewed with suspicion, good intentions easily run into a series of conflicts, and sometimes they have to do with antagonistic mindsets.

According to tertiary education policies in Sierra Leone, private tertiary institutions are not entitled to government subventions. Thus they are self-sponsored, surviving at the expense of tuition fees and the generosities of philanthropists and charities. Against the backdrops of such daunting tasks the proprietors and founders of IAMTECH have paved their way to the top. The institution has enjoyed accelerated development against all odds.

I keep mentioning the civil war because educational ventures, including school buildings, the teaching force and the operation of classes were the hardest hit by the ravages of that war. In that context, it has to be said that certain characteristics came to the fore and made slight but noticeable dents in the national character of the allies, including Great Britain during the war.

Some in Sierra Leone linked up with the RUF rebels and the warring protagonists. These people became thorns in the flesh of the nationalists and patriots like the Kamaras. They posed negative competitions and undermined the efforts of the couples and others who dreamed of similar related ventures. By default or design, they disrupted the smooth running of the projects of private providers. It was a herculean task to say the least for Paul and Paula. They had no choice but get on with it. It was glaring that they had crossed the Rubicon, so there was no turning back.

Again, they were not perturbed as Paula spells out: "We weren't perturbed because we knew that there were those who would compete negatively with the sole aim to derail our project. They spoke ill of our projects even to the extent of disparaging our applications for funding."

Despite all these complex problems, husband and wife didn't give up at all, since it is part of their personality traits. Like determined, seasoned military generals, the couples kept marching the troops forward until they saw light at the end of the tunnel.

Patience is a virtue. It is part of the winning formula through patience and perseverance, they kept the faith. They fought every battle, tooth and nail and tackled every obstacle they encountered until victory dawned.

Paul captured the moments passionately: "In all our efforts, faith in God inspired in us the patience that saw us through. It also made us focused because we know that with the Lord anything is possible!"

His wife echoed the feeling: "We were focused on one fact. That is the post war reconstruction would require preparedness in education, in particular. And the types of skills the country lacks and needs most, among others, are skills in computing and technology"

Surely from faith sprang other virtues and strengths. These attributes made them persist in their endless efforts to succeed. They were extremely focused, so, more often than not they treated some of the obstacles put in their way with a pinch of salt as nothing more than unnecessary distractions that should not be allowed to rock their boats.

Education is an expensive commodity in this part of the world. The partners were virtually a sole business enterprise, meaning that they had to literally fund themselves. Their savings they had when they returned home prior to the civil war soon dried up. In addition to the obstacles highlighted above, the partners had to deal with the demands of customs and traditions. In Africa our customs and traditions stipulate among other things that those who are perceived as well-off in the family whatever the phrase *well-off* means, they are meant to become the breadwinners for the rest of the family. Also, the social word *family* in African traditions and customs does not denote the Western nuclear family but rather an extended family, emphasizing inclusivity at complex levels.

The net impact of these commitments meant that they had to feed, clothe and house members of their extended families. They also had personal friends to care for who had been caught up in difficulties of the war.

There were other important responsibilities they couldn't afford to sweep under the carpet. Otherwise, the very foundations of their belief and faith would plague their consciences. A typical example was the orphans of warfare. The war had left behind thousands of war orphans who needed help. The state made its day-to-day contributions, but the couples had to augment the aid of the state. In some cases, there were no state subsidies to help the vulnerable war orphans, since most of Africa does not enjoy welfare freebies.

"We had to sponsor and finance orphans who had to scratch the surface for themselves and their siblings and friends. We allowed them to attend free classes whilst we had to foot the bills, fetch the salaries of instructors, and pay the rents of the buildings in which we ran classes. We also had to purchase teaching and learning resources," said Dr Mrs Kamara.

By nature, Professor Kamara is a shy and modest character but due to the emotional and sensitive connotations of the subject matter, he was visibly shaken. He reacted instinctively and poured out his innate emotions: "We didn't return home as rich people. But we had duties to perform and perform well, no matter the challenges. Above all, apart from Almighty God, my family and I give priority in all that we do to the service of our fellowmen and our country"

The administrative structure, curriculum contents, qualifications and mode of delivery of lessons are subjects worth reflecting on. When the Kissy Computer Training Institute (KCTI) was founded there was no viable computer training institution in the country.

In fact there were more private typewriter typing pools than computer classes in the city. Besides, most of the private typewriting pools were makeshifts, the size of cubicles. Sierra Leone was far from the internet café age. The picture was worst in the provincial headquarter towns and cities, where there were fewer such opportunities. Besides, the war had destroyed the few old and dilapidated typewriters.

In the mid 1990s coming up to the year 2001 the institution expanded massively and made gains in its overall outputs. The general demographics were inspiring. In terms of students' population, extended learning centeres and the main campus and headquarters at Kissy Dockyards, lecturers and the management and administration, the institution was now showing good signs of growth and stability.

During this period IAMTECH was now proudly talking about a comprehensive structure with the necessary functioning and operational tools in place. This period marked the diversification of the programmes and learning centeres. Classified under various faculties or departments, the programmes were structured to meet the psychosocial, economic, technical; and intellectual needs of students and society at large.

Although it is a private provider, IAMTECH operates within the guidelines of the country's Tertiary Education Commission (TEC). The proprietors are law abiding citizens. They are also disciplined professionals. They can't afford under any circumstances to flout the benchmarks of quality assurance as stipulated by the TEC.

For instance, the entry requirements to all the courses are strictly adhered to at all times. Never has the institution been accused of or found guilty of watering down the quality of education. In a competitive climate in some parts of the world, quality and standards are lowered in order to attract students to courses. Such a culture doesn't exist, nor is it encouraged at IAMTECH.

They say discipline is one of the main keys to success. The discipline regarding enrolment and guiding quality assurance, among other vital policies, are the linchpins for the enormous success stories the institution has built over the years and continues to build. They are enshrined in the policy blueprints of the institution. It comes as no surprise that IAMTECH has become the darling of the nation.

The population of the institution is always on the increase, no matter the usual hiccups that come with growth and development. But whatever comes on their way is treated swiftly by the efficient administrative staff and the academic team. For example, at the matriculation on 14November 2015, despite the ravages of the Ebola epidemic, the number of new students that enrolled on the courses of IAMTECH far exceeded the expectations of the authorities.

In the mid 1990s the institute had built buildings, each with sufficient classrooms for their students' intakes. Since the founding of the institute, the student population has grown from strength to strength. It substantiates one fact, the students and communities the institute serves are happy and satisfied with its overall performance. Their satisfactions and their confidence in the institute have been buttressed by the percentage of the jobs their graduates have secured in the employment sectors of the country.

Not only that there are a lot more gratifying stories worth mentioning. Some graduates progress to further studies in the other institutions, including Njala University, IPAM, Fourah Bay College and Milton Margai as well as in universities abroad. They have also earned senior positions in every facet of our national institutions, both public and private sectors.

The merit of the institution's quality record is clearly spelt out by the actions it has taken in order to maintain standards at all levels of its provisions. It must be said that it has been unfailingly upright and as immaculate as impeccable. All these qualities and many others together have earned the institution and its founders the accolades heaped on them.

Their tenacity energized them all the way, and they have kept the project alive to serve the purpose for which it was established. The manner in which they have achieved their dreams substantiates their success stories.

# PART SIX

# 19

# Rebranding

Did the institution begin with the name IAMTECH? Not according to the archives and founders. It assumed this name as a result of transformation, which required an immediate rebranding. Rebranding is perceived as a means of Innovation.

However, there are always nuances regarding the rationales behind the rebranding of an institution. In this time of stiff competition, rebranding is necessary in order to win the race. It is also dictated by the ambition to achieve excellence and unique qualities that gain recognitions, substantial attractiveness, and accolades. Hence, rebranding is a formidable and forceful tool in this postmodern era.

Rebranding is necessary, no matter the nature and brand of business. It stands out distinctly as the veritable machinery in the business world of marketing and advertising. Educational institutions find it especially necessary to rebrand their outlooks, strategies and rationales.

Also some institutions embark on rebranding in order to refute negative allegations, unfair branding, so as to clean up and regain the confidence of the public. To reiterate institutions of every kind are like products and ideas we need to repackage and promote them effectively in order to stimulate sales. For others rebranding is driven by hunger and ambition for further success. Such success could be epitomized by fame and popularity. Rebranding could be informed by the urgent need to expand current business structures substantially in order to reach a wider customers base.

In addition, institutions are rebranded so that their programmes including distance or e-learning outreach create impact in the nation at large. It is an effective scheme and strategy that restores the liberal values viable educational institutions provide their citizens. In this vein, when educational institutions are rebranded successfully, their services have the capacity to reach the previously unreachable, and they benefit those that have been neglected.

In countries like Sierra Leone, speaking evidentially, this lapse in our education had particularly marred the tertiary level. Indeed, in a good number of academic articles and books academicians have seized upon it as one of the main causes of the civil war. This is not rocket science and there is no need to look elsewhere for any justification whatsoever of this thesis. It is illuminating to reflect on the adage that says an idle mind is an angry mind, and it has the potential to wreak havocs on innocent victims when anger boils over uncontrollably.

Based on all of the above permutations, I discreetly screened the memories of the sole proprietors of the project in order to glean from them the reasons why they changed the name of the institute from Kissy Computer Training Institute to IAMTECH.

Dr Mrs Paula Kamara remarked in a manner more educative than just mere narratives:

"We had to rebrand for obvious reasons. First, we had grown in size and our curriculum was nearing diversification. The institute introduced other courses and qualifications. We were no longer a mere computer institute. We had grown very fast beyond the mediocrity our critics branded us with hitherto"

Over the years students have produced educative and academically informed dissertations and projects. They are in partial fulfilment of the requirements of their qualifications. I went through the rich stores of the institute's library archives and gleaned the following information. It is a glaring argument and manifestation of the need for rebranding.

It reads succinctly: "Initially the computer technology course was designed as a general certificate course in computer studies."

Then the literature goes on to narrate further: "As the demand for computer literacy increased, the institution thought it wise to add to its curriculum software packages, and academic studies like office procedures, accounting, statistics, communication skills, and French among others. The centre gained recognition from the Ministry of Education as the first viable institution in these directions in 1994"

Thus, the rebranding was informed by increase in the number of courses other than computer study skills. Curriculum diversification was the inspiration. The other reasons were equally important. Not only did they have the internal approval of the national education authorities they were also granted external recognition and accreditations from various universities and professional institutions. This earned the institute an international clout.

The institute was renamed and rebranded Institute of Advanced Management and Technology, abbreviated as IAMTECH. These changes in the existence of the institution were enough to engineer a wholesale rebranding or what others refer to as renaming.

Another dissertation elaborated on the rebranding cleverly as follows: "In 1996, the centre was accredited and upgraded to an institute (IAMTECH). Within the same academic year, the institute gained a franchise agreement within Generic Computer School, Singapore, which automatically linked it with Chico University (California) and Manchester Metropolitan University (UK)"

Powering through his narrative, the author injected self-acclaim for the lofty achievements of his beloved IAMTECH: "Thus IAMTECH became the cradle of Distance Learning in Sierra Leone" In this context, the proprietors were arguably determined to give IAMTECH international clout as a provider of a mixture of curricula that would elevate it at par with the very best within and outside Sierra Leone. It is the only tertiary institution in the country where lecturers teach with the aid of smart boards. It is quite a breathtaking innovative method of learning.

The institute offered off-campus undergraduate degree programmes. They ranged from accounting and finance, administration, human resources and procurement to development studies and computer science and technology. IAMTECH now had the capacity to train Sierra Leoneans and immigrants from the sub-Sahara region in order to address the region's manpower needs.

These innovations took place at the right time. Sierra Leone was emerging from warfare, so qualifications in information technology and computer science were needed to rebuild the war torn nation. Prior to this period, the country was stuck in old disciplines which had outlived their usefulness, socioeconomically speaking. Students at other universities read degree courses including Greek and Roman cultural history, which didn't offer much in terms of relevance for employment, except for the novelty. At face values, these disciplines are academically relevant, but even the very founding antecedents Britain, of Sierra Leone's educational system have moved on. For decades now the focus has been on job related skills and educational acquisitions.

The curricula contents of most disciplines in the industrialized countries are now designed to reflect the realities of the world of employment. Government policies have been reviewed over and over to reflect the demands and requirements of the job market. These changes and reforms were exacerbated by the economic crises in the late 1970s and 80s during the premiership of the late British prime minister, Mrs Margaret Thatcher. Since then emphasis have been weighed heavily in favour of the significance and economic values of vocational and pure and applied science courses. The romantic feelings and novelty associated with the liberal arts subjects are losing their ascendency among curriculum designers as well as policymakers in this day and age.

# 20

# Boundless Ideas

The discipline and great ideas that have been in vogue in Britain and elsewhere since the late 1980s are definitely those that have sought the answers to their pressing socioeconomic challenges of the time. Middleman power courses are relevant for creating jobs and wealth for societies. These great and boundless ideas are productive because they are game changers in terms of economic development. It means that higher educational institutions can't afford to design curricula in isolation these days. They cannot educate communities and society at large in isolation from persistent socioeconomic challenges.

The new commercial and vocational disciplines alleviate poverty and computer science and technology enable societies to grow and alert to the day-to day political, social and economic events of the world. The grip social media has on the information world is too exciting and profound for any educational institutions or governments to ignore. It is self-evident that a war torn country such as Sierra Leone requires disciplines, skills and qualifications that are relevant to socioeconomic development and guarantees political stability.

As they grew more in confidence, the new changes in the life of IAMTECH called for the urgent need to recruit more qualified and professionally experienced staff. There were now sufficient classrooms. The library and relevant teaching and learning resources were upgraded in order to meet the required national and international standards.

Since IAMTECH was now aligned to internal and external accreditation bodies and universities, it had to meet all their requirements. The next step was to update their quality assurance and audit portfolios regularly. Their external partners paid regular visits, sometimes unannounced. Since they had no skeletons in the cupboards to hide, the proprietors and academic faculties invited their partners to come and do their jobs. They were at virtually every matriculation and convocation ceremony of the institute. Their external partners on sabbatical leave took up lectureship and research endeavours. They meticulously assessed the provisions of the institution as required by the official stipulations of the partnership modalities.

Education is one of the most expensive projects, whether owned by government or privately. It has always been a herculean task to say the least, to operate a private institution of the calibre and magnitude of IAMTECH. Determined and ambitious as the Kamaras are, it is always business as usual for them. Come rain or sunshine, they are determined, and their nationalist and patriotic instincts kick against any manner of temptation.

They elaborated on these crucial points: "Education at this level is not for profit making. In England, education at the tertiary level is a charitable organization, which makes it extremely expensive. Even in the case when government used to give grants-in-aid, the expenses involved in running educational institutions still posed a lot of challenges. Those of us who lived in England during the Conservative era are very much aware of the financial challenges that schools, colleges and universities encountered in the hands of the Iron Lady Margaret Thatcher. Driven by privatization and her determination to reduce the size of the state and expenditure, she cut everything, ranging from manual workers to academicians"

It was not only the Conservatives that injected hell into the educational system in Britain. The advent of Tony Blair's New Labour Party did not help the system either. Teaching jobs and research capital were cut drastically, as were grants- in- aid for universities.

Tony Blair deviated completely from the traditional Left's agenda of the Old Labour Party. In his Third Way trend and policy shift, he replaced the old policies and embarked on a new form of privatization. As an unpopular policy, it was demeaned and called "privatization through the backdoor" by the late veteran Old Labour politician Tony Ben. The scheme was known as the public-private partnership (PPP). In fact it accelerated the massive financial problems in the public sector of Britain.

Rebranding and renaming were both a blessing in disguise and one of the greatest challenges the administrators of IAMTECH have to deal with to this day. Despite all the enduring challenges, they have not been perturbed to apply their brakes on expanding the institution further. It is obvious clients clamour to gain admission at the institution.

So what is it that continues to attract them to this institution? The general answer hinges on the quality of education they offer. The specific answer is that unlike the other tertiary institutions, IAMTECH charges reasonable fees. They also apply flexibility to the payment of the fees. In other institutions, students go through many hassles in order to pay their tuition fees. Not only that, but measures are put in place for defaulters. The measures include banning them from attending lecturers until they pay up.

The sad thing about such strictures is that by the time students scrape through and pay up, they will have missed substantial periods of their lectures. Here at IAMTECH, it is quite the opposite. Students enjoy the compassion that comes with the kindness and patriotism of the founders. In view of the rate of poverty in the country and many other related socioeconomic problems which come with poverty, defaulters are allowed reasonable time to pay up their tuition fees whilst they continue to attend lectures.

Wherever have you heard that students pay their remaining balance fees on the very day before their convocation ceremony? There is no other institution in the land that allows that but IAMTECH. Why? The philosophy of the institution underscores the flexibilities enjoyed by the staff, students, employers and communities the institution serves.

Abie Paula Amphithearter

Administrative And Academic Staff

Dr Lauretta Will Sillah- Principal

Dr. James Obai Fullah- Dean- Students Affairs

Dr. (Mrs) Abie Paula Kamara- Foundind Chairperson

Dr. Michael Nicolas Mundah- Vice Principal Administrative Affairs

Finance Department

Front View With Administrative Building Under Construction

Graduation Ceremony 2015 (2)

Graduation Ceremony 2015 (3)

Lab 1

Prof. Dr. Paul Kamara Ceo And Founding Chairperson

Prof. Patrick F. U. Taylor-Vice Principal Academic Affairs

Students On Exams

# 21

# IAMTECH's Philosophy

The motto of the institute is couched in an eye-catching phrase. It is boldly inscribed on the front page of its prospectus. It reads "For Country and For Humanity" This motto underscores the philosophy of the core values it stands for. True to what is a solemn vow, since its inception, IAMTECH has pursued these core values vigorously to the letter.

Let us make sense of the philosophy which is at the centre of this motto both philosophically and through its wider benefits. Literally "for country and for humanity" simply means rendering service to humans and country.

In the United Kingdom, for example, there is a popular cliché which underpins the nationalist belief and spirit of the Brits. It is "for Queen and Country" The ordinary interpretation means sacrifice in the name of Her Royal Highness, Her Majesty the Queen, Queen Elizabeth. It has to do with service to the nation state of the United Kingdom.

In a similar vein, members of British Armed Forces go to war in defence of the British monarchy and the country. They also go to war in defence of the British Commonwealth. The government of the United Kingdom and the Commonwealth serves the interests of United Kingdom and the Commonwealth.

The philosophy of IAMTECH resonates such inferences, but it is principally about humanist interpretations. The virtues of love, service, dedication, and sacrifice for human values as well as the country of which anyone is a bona fide national constitute the backbones of the philosophy.

It has to do with how these values inform the rationales, aims and objectives of the programmes the institute offers. They will help us in the direction of understanding its philosophy.

Another important trajectory is the relationships between the institute and the communities they serve. They come into play because social instruments, including educational institutions can't operate in isolation from the communities they serve. In total, how the services, the community relations, and the programmes of IAMTECH, in general, impact and affect humanity and country at large, form the bulwarks of this philosophy.

Therefore, the intent of IAMTECH's motto is to hammer home the philosophy that its own rationale of tertiary education is all about serving the interests of humanity in communities and the entire country.

Reflecting on the eye-catching phrase "for country and for humanity" which is the main kernel of the philosophy of the institution, over the years it has practiced the inherent values. Take the programmes it offers for instance. They are versatile, in the sense that they provide the vitally needed knowledge, skills and qualifications. In addition to which, they also mould students to emulate and practice good behaviour and character in the concrete service of their fellow citizens as well as their communities.

These values are enshrined in the students' handbook or prospectus. The rules and principal guidelines are instructive to lecturers, students, wards, and parents. They form the cornerstones of the social contract that binds the students and the institute's authorities. Whilst the institute protects and seeks the interests of the students, the students on their part should abide by the disciplinary codes of the institute.

Serving communities is vital among the features which define the philosophy of IAMTECH. There is evidence that the relationship between the institution and its communities is extremely healthy. In addition to the relevance of their programmes healthy community, it ensures that both college authorities and students establish and support community initiatives. They have become unique norms and values among IAMTECH's students.

IAMTECH's proud alumni association is very active in support of community programmes which bring people together. The current students' canteen in the main campus was set up through alumni initiatives.

The relation also inspires and nurtures a strong virtue of caring. Members contribute to the capital projects of the institute. The classrooms and library projects at the Kono campus were built by students. In addition to their own personal financial and material contributions, they raised funds from the wider community in the Kono District. The strong, community relations have boosted the demographics.

The new intakes are always healthy. Whilst some of her counterparts suffer from low enrolments, the institute's programmes are always oversubscribed. This is due to two factors. The programmes are relevant and attractive to potential employers. Also, they have become popular over the decades due to the combinations of warm community relations and the popularity of their teaching staff.

In addition to the knowledge and skills values of the institute's philosophy, the political values are important. Sierra Leone is a heterogeneous society, with different cultures, political affiliations, religions, and traditions of the different ethnicities.

At IAMTECH differences are recognized and respected. However, it is an inclusive college, which provides for everyone regardless of differences in culture, ethnicity and religion. The composition of the entire staff and promotion policy reflects heterogeneity as a vital piece of its philosophy.

The proprietors were keen to offer comments on their views of the institute's philosophy. I started first with Professor Paul Kamara. "Our philosophy embraces an all-inclusive service to humanity and country. Our work is for the good and betterment of the fellowman and our country. We don't do anything that only serves our interests. This institute bears neither the name of one of our family members nor my wife and me"

His wife, Dr Mrs Paula Kamara was even more eloquent on the issue. "Our country has encountered some serious setbacks to the extent that our national development dwindled. It is simply due to the fact that we have not been faithful to the good causes. Most of the faults lie with tertiary institutions. They have not been inclusive enough. This was what inspired my husband and me to set up IAMTECH. The reason is to inspire and practice these values"

I asked her to explain further.

"We established a scholarship programmes for the needy, even though we receive little or no government subvention the mainstream institutions do. We believe that an institution can only be of value if it serves humanity and country"

That IAMTECH's courses and their qualifications have empowered graduates to put food on their tables and afford clothing and shelter means it is project that works in the interests of humanity. Graduates of IAMTECH are employed in various sectors of Sierra Leone, meanings they are serving their country.

The graduates of this great institution serve in the police force, prisons and corrections service. They also serve the Sierra Leone Army. These useful services have cemented service to their country.

It is undoubtedly the case that both the authorities and students have attained milestones since 1991. They have pursued the motto and the enlightened philosophy of the institute to the letter.

# 22

# Milestones

Affiliation of tertiary educational institutions, like autonomous accreditation status, involves tedious and challenging processes in most of Africa. The Sierra Leone procedures are not peculiar at all and it is an open secret that in Sierra Leone they are not free of politics and high dramas. More often than not the procedures run into obstacles of implicit and explicit machinations that have nothing to do with academic and professional criteria.

The year 2010 marked an incredible milestone in the history of IAMTECH. It was in that year that it became affiliated with Njala University. Njala University is one of the constituent colleges under the umbrella of the University of Sierra Leone. Years ago when Njala was not part of this umbrella arrangement, it was known as Njala University College.

The implications of this policy speak volumes in real terms. The policy is both political and professional, although critics have other views. I am of the view that the policy creates a demarcation between the elite tertiary education institutions that operate under this official umbrella and the ones that are not accorded the right to be among the constituent colleges of the University of Sierra Leone. It therefore implies that although IAMTECH has commanded such profound pedigree and academic capital since its inception, it has not been considered as one of the elite institutions in the country yet.

That raises the question. Does this implication diminish IAMTECH's real academic stature and all the successes it has built over the two decades? It does not, because the populace is very much aware that the real issues that count are quality and relevance of the courses the institution offers. They are aware of the pertinent reality that IAMTECH is a force to reckon with in all aspects that develop and promote an aspiring nation. Two decades and a half since it was established, the institution may not be acknowledged as an elite institution with the proverbial social status, but it has its own great, popular appeal in the country.

Most important, Sierra Leoneans are gratified to acknowledge that it has proved its mettle in terms of the ideal and relevant, economically viable, job oriented programmes it offers and the general philosophy it espouses and practices at large.

The affiliation between the two institutions is mutually beneficial, economically and socially. On one hand Njala University appends its seal of office and accreditation awarded to all the students that meet the prescribed criteria. The administration at IAMTECH also enjoys the accolade that it derives from the seal Njala appends on the compendiums of her graduates.

On top of that Njala serves as external examiners for IAMTECH and it has to certify all grades before they are declared as pass, distinction or fail. It also approves the courses that IAMTECH offers. Above all the collaborative arrangements boost the social pedigree of Njala University, adding leverage to its academic and demographic clouts.

An academician summed up the affiliation's arrangements and implications:

"Theoretically, Njala is acknowledged as an autonomous university that manages another institution. That institution operates under its auspices and seal of approval without which it can't afford to take the risk and operate and award qualifications approved by the TEC. Its seal of approval has the blessings of the TEC and therefore the constitution of the land. The approval it gives for all of these functions and more to IAMTECH entails expenses. Significantly, they add more values to the social status and its size and population as one of the elite institutions in the land with affiliate institutions. On the other hand, as the beneficiary of the affiliation, IAMTECH's compendiums are accredited as valid and therefore the recipients are entitled to all the benefits and privileges which go with the weight of their awards. It also means that they are by implication part and parcel of the social status and respectability that defines the status of Njala University. Theoretically, Njala also has a seat on the Tertiary Education Commission (TEC), directorates on behalf of IAMTECH and by virtue of its own status as an autonomous university. It literally means that the fate and destiny of IAMTECH rests not in its own hands but those of Njala University"

As expected, the mutual relationship between the institutions has not been easy sailing. They have both converged as well as diverged over issues. The reasons for the divergences are obvious. The two institutions differ more than they are alike in terms of culture and institutional arrangements. By far the older in the business after FBC was founded in 1827 Njala University has enjoyed university status and privileges which are otherwise out of reach for IAMTECH.

Njala University like FBC enjoys maximum subventions which offset its management expenses, in addition to the grants-in-aid which its students enjoy. IAMTECH is a sole business venture that survives at the expense of student fees and donations from former students' associations, members of the communities it serves and other well wishers who appreciate the good works it does.

Significantly, due to its age and autonomy, Njala University enjoys much greater social status than IAMTECH. Comparatively, IAMTECH is a little known institution and therefore has a handful of people and sympathizers in high places. Its alumni population is far less than that of Njala University which has existed for decades.

In fact but for the relevance of its programmes and the philosophy it espouses, IAMTECH would have remained in the periphery of the consciousness of Sierra Leoneans. Sierra Leoneans are by nature a conservative breed and change is not often an attractive phenomenon for them. Most people in the population are more in tune with the history and physical presence of the two universities FBC and NU than all the other tertiary institutions, including IAMTECH.

Apart from that, the political elites, educationalists, technocrats and the wealthy and powerful in high places officially recognize and appreciate the two elite universities more than they do IAMTECH. Historically the relationships tertiary institutions have had with the political class over the decades have become ominously cultic in nature and diversity. Most of the elite institutions are connected to members of the high society through social organization or fraternities. These cultures are not peculiar to Sierra Leone. Similar trends prevail in other African countries, the United States of America and the United Kingdom.

The Old Boy fetishism is hard at work in most of Africa. Consider Ghana and Nigeria, Legon in Ghana and Abeokuta and Ile Ife in Nigeria characterize nothing other than a cult system in which unbroken lifelong loyalties surpass all other considerations.

You may wonder whether IAMTECH prefers to remain yoked to Njala University or to break free. The word or concept break free is inappropriate in this context, but it constitutes the layman's point of view. The answer is absolutely no as nobody cooperates with or enjoys bondage. Freedom is priceless which is why IAMTECH relishes autonomous university status, like any other affiliate institution of the two elite universities. Documented evidences in the archives of its convocations ceremonies attest that this great institution has made it abundantly clear that it craves for accredited autonomous university status.

As one of numerous living witnesses, I have served at their convocation ceremonies on three occasions as public orator. Each time, the principal of IAMTECH has lauded the institution's ambition to gain independent university status in her speech. So did her predecessor, Dr Mrs Abie Paula Kamara. Their appeals, calls and pronouncements have fallen on deaf ears. They always received the loudest of applause from both the invited guests of honour and students. Successive Students Union Presidents have lent their voices to this important, historic quest as well.

It is an undisputed fact that IAMTECH has the inherent legitimacy like others before and after it to aspire to autonomous accredited university status. One is constrained to revisit a key point made earlier about the high politics surrounding the granting of university status to tertiary colleges in the land. In as much as the professionals and experts at the TEC often guide the rules and regulations governing accreditation jealously, there are limits to their zealousness.

Here are some selected comments made by concerned citizens regarding the subject of granting university status by the TEC. A retired academician commented: "TEC has problems which are not necessarily of their making. They have well educated, experienced and respectable chairman and directors. But, in my view, some of their problems are borne out of default, over which they have no control or say. They are constrained by the poisonous culture of arms-twisting by people from the very top of the system. Still they have done a very good job over the years by reforming the sector"

The comments of this academician are on the lips of every analyst within and outside the country with cares and concerns about the status of the tertiary sector in Sierra Leone. For example, a renowned Sierra Leonean educationist now retired made these salient points: "The TEC is one of the few good things that have ever happened to the history of tertiary education in this country. Unfortunately, more often than not, their good intentions are handicapped by the political class, misconstrued by some people"

There is another view contrary to the two views expressed above as follows: "IAMTECH is one of the up and growing tertiary institutions in the private sector in this country that has done extremely well. They teach well and have very relevant programmes from which most people have gained enormously and secured well paid jobs. It has a vibrant, committed staff and founders. We know they are clamouring for autonomous university status. However, in my view, they need to put things in order, and then they will be ready for it in the near future"

Like most of my colleagues, I do reckon that the entire team of the institution at IAMTECH does appreciate the affiliation with NU. However the college craves for autonomous accredited university status because of one golden aspiration shared by all of humanity independent status. The benefits which accrue from an autonomous status by far surpass pupillage and affiliation. It makes sense that the team believes that autonomous university status is the sure means of sustaining legitimate claims to sovereignty. It will galvanize all the gains and achievements it has made since its inception.

# 23

# Capital Projects

It is a miraculous leap of faith that a self-sponsored educational institution such as IAMTECH will undertake the number of capital projects it has undertaken. The beauty is that it manifests the industry, hard work and determination of the founders.

It is true that over the years, there has been a spectacular proliferation of private colleges and universities in the continent of Africa. However, the downside of this surge in the private sector provision is that most private higher educational institutions in this populous continent operate in rented buildings. IAMTECH is a different phenomenon altogether. Apart from the Circular Road, YWCA and Bo Learning Centeres, the rest of the facilities, including the main campus in Kissy Dockyards, Freetown Lunsar, Rokupr, Kambia and Kono are owned by the founders. Thanks to the hardworking, seriousness of the leader of the Bo Leaning Centre, the new structures were at wall heights towards the end of 2015. The classrooms are almost close to completion and the sporting spaces are the delights of any postmodern building craftsmanship.

The Bo project is not only symbolic it speaks of a rationale which cannot be ignored easily. IAMTECH has been consistent about this rationale as the working zeal and mechanisms of its capital projects and projects around the country. First, when education reaches those with little or no access in societies that are less developed, then it has made its mark on the rest of society. IAMTECH is pursuing this philosophy with vigour because of its national benefits.

Successive governments have made great efforts to curb and even eliminate illiteracy in the country but there have been serious handicaps. Above all, Sierra Leone's situation has become precarious considering the challenges it has endured recently the civil war, the Ebola epidemic and the floods. These calamities have yoked us to foreign dependency culture dwarfing or diminishing our sovereignty and stature in the eyes of the world. In this light, the pains that come with our persistent dependency constrained

IAMTECH to take up the challenge and break that chain of dependency that has yoked the nation to foreign facilitators and consultants for disciplines such as procurement of oil and gas, which some of these learning centres offer. It is also about prestige, respectability and honour. The learning centeres outside the city of Freetown are landmark edifices that give respectability to IAMTECH as a viable institution and signs that it has come to stay for good.

The capital projects also have a commercial value. They constitute one of the key selling points of the college and draw more students into its fold. That our admissions growths have grown so enormously justifies the rationale behind these capital projects. The aesthetic meanings are superb beyond descriptions giving architectural meaning and beauty to the structures. How many times have we not heard our student population and their friends and loved ones refer to the beauty and massiveness of IAMTECH's learning centres especially the twelve floor skyscraper that is under construction currently at the headquarters campus in Kissy Dockyards? It is amazing!

Read these comments by one of the many admirers of the college: "Over the years these projects and the quality of programmes IAMTECH runs have marketed the college and have attracted more students each year to its courses. The adage is that learners are often enticed by the structures which house them. The magnificence of the buildings and classrooms in which learning takes place has a lot of advantages. Massive, beautifully built edifices inspire students because they are all about creating a comfortable learning environment"

The capital invested in massive beautiful edifices is important, but it shows the ability of the owners to be consistent with repairs and maintenance. How often and regularly the buildings are renovated and kept to maximum quality standards actually matters, among other things. Some institutions do struggle with issues of maintenance and renovations of their buildings. That is not the case with IAMTECH. Repairs and maintenance are always carried out so as to maintain the beauty and solidity of the properties. The institution has an estate officer who ensures that the buildings are well kept.

IAMTECH is also concerned about keeping the environment healthy and habitable. It has a committed team of builders, some of who are job placed as interns at the centre in order to have viable practical experience. Students come first in whatever the college conceives to undertake by way of development. Hence the architects of these capital projects put students at the centre of the operational plans. Students are always wary of taking lessons in classrooms or buildings wrapped in spider webs or infested by mice which can expose the learners as well as instructors to health hazards.

Most of these buildings have withstood the test of time. They were solidly built on strong pillars and foundations which is why they have averted any form of accident or health and safety problems since they were constructed. The new ones under construction are given similar considerations. The major capital projects that will remain the landmark symbols of IAMTECH are the main campus building, the European Hall, the Student Canteen buildings, the administrative buildings and the Abie Paula Amphitheatre.

There is one important experience I have had regarding the behaviours of humanity. My late parents always reminded me about what it means and takes to live an incredible and productive way of life. My dad would say to me now and again: "My son, always keep on your toes and work hard even without immediate rewards or praises. Be a good soldier, and soldier on at all times, for one fine day, the good Lord will surely send your own Samaritan to come to your aid"

I believe that the couple must have had similar admonitions from their parents which have kept them soldiering on, from sunrise to sunset. Although they are neither entitled to massive government subventions nor to external aid like the other old institutions, yet once in a while, good Samaritans do come to their aid.

The aid they receive as voluntary gestures comes in the forms of community aid, philanthropists and goodwill ambassadors. It is from such generosity that they have been able to augment the contents of their own personal purse and build these gallant structures.

Typical products of these goodwill gestures are the structures in Kono. They were constructed as a result of part-sponsorships from the local communities as well as sponsorships and gifts from both their students and other generous people. Whatever degree of private financial and material support the family had had, they literally financed these capital projects from the proceeds of tuition fees.

The encouraging and motivating bit about the local support they are given from time to time is that it underscores the local ownership of the project. It is also the prototype of the mini public-private partnership that has gone a long way to define the perceptions and opinions about the very communities that IAMTECH serves.

The nexus between the world of teaching and the world of computer science and technology has grown beyond all doubt to become unbreakable. We are living in the twenty-first century, so the days of chalks, slates, and blackboards and overhead projectors are over. Classroom practices are now enhanced in this day and age by electronic, interactive white boards.

With the exception of IAMTECH, there is no educational institution, including universities, polytechnics, colleges and all tiers of the pre-tertiary institution that uses electronic interactive smart boards to teach or lecture in the country. It means that we are behind in treble digits and we are playing catch up. By the beginning of the next academic year, plans have been made to add more to these new, postmodern gadgets of teaching and learning. It is one of the many capital investments projects that will bring more enlightenment spirit to the learning atmosphere of IAMTECH.

The beauty of IAMTECH's projects is that they have inspired foreign investors to augment the efforts of the proprietors. Recently a technology company based abroad donated free solar energy Internet and computer gadgets to the institution's school of technology. The gadgets have attracted more new entrants. Besides IAMTECH is one of the few tertiary institutions that can boast of an Internet and computer laboratory.

Here at this college, the use of computers and the Internet is compulsory. All students are supposed to undertake a complete IT course of studies in addition to their main disciplines. This policy has immense benefits, because by the time they complete their certificate, diploma and degree courses, they know how to practically use modern information technology. This is an ideal policy for educational pursuits in post-war Sierra Leone.

This is not in any way an attempt to cast aspersions on the other institutions because they have made their marks and still continue to do so in other disciplines. Besides, IAMTECH is aware that it has just been introduced as a new comer on the scene of higher education in Sierra Leone. Therefore, it only makes sense for it to be ambitious, adventurous and innovative in order to make up the grounds that the elite institutions have covered over the years. The zeal and ambitions of IAMTECH to continue and make inroads into the inaccessible regions of Sierra Leone, taking relevant skills and qualifications to them so that their people are strengthened through its determination to empower people.

The founders of this ambitious and most successful institutions in post-war Sierra Leone are conscious of the Chinese adage: "The sun shines on those who stand before it shines on those who kneel before them" By way of reiteration, all the stakeholders of IAMTECH are very much aware that the institution is young and it is a private provider, so it must constantly redouble its efforts in order to catch up with the old and elite institutions.

# 24

# Distance Learning

The distance education programmes at IAMTECH has not only gained tremendous prominence and popularity. Like the mining, petroleum, oil and gas courses, it is the institution's forte. This institution is proud to be the first in the land to offer these new courses which have become household names and attracted students the more.

There is no need to stress the significance and viability of this model of acquiring skills and qualifications. Generally speaking, this method of delivering lectures at the doorsteps of the learners with ease has commanded tremendous attention in the discourse analysis of modern day education.

There is every good reason this is so. Let me take you down memory lane and you will agree with me. According to a report published by the Working Group on Distance Education and Open Learning in Sub-Saharan Africa in 2012, there is a great potential for distance education to contribute to the provision of education for all. Distance education programs offer the opportunity for education and learning to reach the unreachable.

Not only that but this method makes it possible for the disaffected to be given the second chance to fulfil their potential. In most of the Third World, including Africa, with Sierra Leone as no exception, the school dropout rate is high. Some children are left behind in the first instance because of lack of capital or the absence of a school for them to attend. The same scenario applies to Sierra Leone situation in relation to the limited opportunities to acquire higher education.

What is distance education, you might ask? The meanings associated with this model of learning have become wide ranging. I will stick to this version which makes absolute sense because the underlying logic is sound. By distance education, I mean that method of delivering training and education to students with minimal direct contact between teachers and learners.

The admiration of distance education in Sierra Leone has been cemented especially in the post civil war years. However, learning through distance is not new to Sierra Leone. Distance education schemes such as the Rapid Results College and Wolsey Hall courses were some of the most popular modes of distance education which started in the early years of education in the country and lasted for decades before the advent of the conflict.

For the best part of 1950s and the 1980s, most people couldn't gain admission to Fourah Bay College mostly due to the bottleneck problems. The only alternative was that those who could afford it, enrolled on ordinary and advanced levels for the General Certificate of Education (GCE), in as well as degree courses offered through distance by the Rapid Results College and Wolsey Hall. They were some of the private distance learning institutions in the United Kingdom.

However, these courses didn't necessarily meet the aspirations of the national demands, and the reasons ranged from lack of affordable fees to the distance between providers and the recipients or students. Learning resources didn't reach most of the unreachable. For instance, most aspiring students that lived in the remote areas of the country encountered problems to enrol on the course. In the twenty-first century, thankfully, Sierra Leone has put most of these constraints behind her for many years.

Distance education has not only been popularized but it has become officially recognized by the national legislature. With the Education Act Section 1 of 2004, the Sierra Leone Parliament enacted it into law. I must appeal for caution for ratifying it does not mean that this model of education has become affordable for all aspirants in the country.

IAMTECH has embraced this model and its values because the inherent strategies are centered on the interests of learners. The teaching staff members at IAMTECH have tailored the course in such a way that they are not subject-centered. They give preference to learners and their needs are catered for meticulously. The institution offers distance learning at all of its learning centres within and beyond the city of Freetown.

The centeres at which the courses are offered include the Bo, Kambia, Kono, Rokupr and Lunsar Learning Centres. The courses are the same as the ones taught at the headquarters in Freetown, Circular Road and YWCA

Learning Centres. The only difference is the mode of delivery. Lectures and other activities which are not distance learning models are taught through direct, face-to-face contacts between the lecturers and students.

Regarding distance learning or correspondence learning, lectures are delivered from the local centeres and headquarters through the institute's sophisticated computer and information technology channels and outfits. The duties of the local learning centres are augmented by heads of department and deans at the head office. The programs are supervised by a director of distance learning, who is also Dean of Students of the institution. His duties include the coordination and supervision of the programmes in addition to his general duties as the dean of the entire student body at IAMTECH.

We need to remind ourselves that some of the misgivings about this mode of learning are baseless. Critics often say quality is compromised, watered down or that learning and teaching are of low quality. The IAMTECH model is of the highest quality. The courses are underpinned by the values of quality assurance in terms of delivery, assessment and coordination and management.

General quality and productivity of the programmes are crowned by the endless benefits learners as well as the institution in general enjoy. Here are some of the many advantages distance learning brings to the learning and teaching communities in general: (i.) candidates learn in their own time; (ii) the approach minimizes cost and it is cost effective as the quality of the skills acquired backed by the qualifications are viable; (iii.) candidates have the freedom to set their own personal goals through a well defined and carefully thought through individual learning plan scheme (ILP). The plan is designed by both the lecturers and the students with targets and regular reviews dates set accordingly.

Students are instructed carefully and inspired to take responsibility for the sound and beneficial development of their own academic, intellectual and social skills. Individual responsibility to achieve and perfect skills is tested by the course coordinators at regular intervals during their individual learning plans reviews. Above all when students fully acquire the skills, they are in good stead to meet the complex challenges in life. Their attitudes, behaviour and characters have been well moulded to the optimum as refined and responsible citizens.

The director of the distance learning programme and Dean of Students at IAMTECH is Dr Obai Fullah. He is a seasoned coordinator of this model of learning. He is credited with restructuring the curriculum of distance education at the college. Commenting on the programme he threw some salient lights on its nature and management and the successes it has achieved since it was introduced in the college.

"The distance learning programme isn't necessarily the miracle that will cure all the ills in our educational provisions. However what it is capable of doing is to create the awareness of education further deep in their consciousness. It will also ease some of the pressures at the heart of the traditional style of delivering lessons to learners in classrooms"

"Here at IAMTECH the distance learning program is one of the college's innovative schemes. It is spreading and gaining momentum gradually in the country. What we need to do is to maximize the gains we have made through massive investment in the programmes. This institution is a private provider, and one of the hurdles it faces is funding. The governments and political parties of all colours should invest in this model. As leader of one of the political parties in our country, my main objective is to utilize the forum of education through distance education in particular in order to emphasize a key message. That is if we invest in open and distance learning we shall succeed in taking education to our people, the deprived masses in our rural communities"

During the last semester Dr Fullah was away in the UK. In his place we had a coordinator in the person of Mr Conteh. Lending his voice to the general performance of the programme so far, he alluded to the wider benefits of the open and distance learning course offered by IAMTECH and how it has changed the complexities of the channels through which education could be achieved.

Mr Conteh emphasized that the arenas of teaching and learning have assumed different dimensions. That is to say, gone are the days when teaching and learning were one dimensional. Gone are the days when students earned education only in classrooms and through the face-to-face delivery method. Today teaching comes in all shapes and forms and they are effective as well as accessible to multitudes in our remote communities.

# PART SEVEN

# 25

# Learning Centres

IAMTECH is not only found in Freetown. There are learning centres in almost all the interior of the country. There is an interesting nexus between learning centres and distance learning. While some learning centres offer distance learning programmes others don't. But distance learning is the dream of every learning centre because of its innovative learning advantages and benefits.

I have highlighted the number of learning centres that are run by IAMTECH. There are three centres in Freetown the main campus, which is also the headquarters at the Kissy Dockyards, Circular Road and the Young Women's Christian Association (YWCA). In the interior, there are learning centres at Bo, Kono, Kambia, Rokupr and Lunsar.

It would be an exaggeration to state that these learning centres are excellently equipped with all the equipment and resources they need. Generally speaking, learning resources are always in short supply, geopolitical differences notwithstanding. Even in the most sophisticated, advanced, and rich countries in the world there have always been rifts between teaching professionals and governments and other education stakeholders over resources and pay.

The scarcity of resources is also due to the fact that learning and knowledge are always evolving. The reason for this scarcity is simple. Knowledge is not the development of resources all the time. Their pursuit is the nightmare of administrators and governments.

The administrative structures of IAMTECH's learning centres in Freetown and in rural areas have the freedom to operate within the prescribed guidelines supplied from the main campus. For instance, dissertations and related projects are supervised by the coordinators, deans and heads of departments based at the main campus. This administrative principle applies more to students enrolled on the distance learning programmes.

There are enormous advantages which accrue from the college's diversification project. As I have stated before, the advantages come in different shapes and forms. Cleverly, some of the learning centres are strategically located. Kambia and Rokupr are currently operating more or less as combined centres due to domestic, political reasons that are not pertinent to the theme of this book.

However what is ideal to comment on is that there are clarion calls from the two sister communities to treat them as separate entities. Whether these calls will be heeded remains to be seen and lies within the judgement of the founders and proprietors. The strategic advantages of the two centres are glaringly attractive. In fact I would argue that they are too tempting to ignore. No business strategist would ignore the enormous benefits which could be gained from such locations. The two townships are so close to the Guinea border that one could easily stroll into the Republic of Guinea in less than half an hour during the dry season.

The same ease of travelling prevails during the raining season. Passengers are ferried across in local canoes and boats from Kambia in Sierra Leone into Guinea. Getting as many numbers as possible, constitutes one of the realistic targets of private educational institutions. IAMTECH is no exception to this reality for it is a reasonable way of doing business. The potentials of enrolling students from Guinea in hefty numbers are every proprietor's dream or ambition.

Amazingly, the advantages of this strategic location benefit both countries. When Guineans acquire qualifications from IAMTECH learning centres in Kambia and Rokupr, they are exposed to a lot of advantages. They secure jobs and learn the English oriented culture. They may have the opportunity to settle in Sierra Leone or even acquire Sierra Leonean citizenship.

Sierra Leonean nationals too have the opportunity to become bilingual. They may maximize the competitive advantages of learning a second language. In the process IAMTECH assumes a bilingual profile internationally.

In addition to the economic advantages IAMTECH stands to gain from the strategic location of the sites at Rokupr and Kambia, there are other benefits. The social benefits which are centered on cultural exchange and education are vital for social cohesion between nations. The Republics of Guinea and Liberia are our sister neighbouring states with which we have had ages of political and historical ties that bind three countries. Some of the ethnic groups found in Sierra Leone are in all three countries.

In fact history tells us that these ethnic groups have a lot in common. There is even a contentious argument that had these ties been strengthened enough, the rebel incursions from Liberia wouldn't have taken place.

To reiterate the points made before regarding this subject matter, IAMTECH is keen on spreading its learning facilities throughout Sierra Leone. The main reason justifies the values of the motto. This humanitarian motto is the cornerstone of the philosophy of the founders and proprietors. Since these parts of the country where the college is located came into existence, some of them have never had a tertiary institution. Hence the symbolic significance is whether knowingly or otherwise, IAMTECH has made a political point.

The politics which it professes is nationalism, underpinned by patriotism. A true nationalist and patriot is keen to serve his or her compatriots at large regardless of regional and social differences or divergent ethnicity or religion. And it is fair to state that these beliefs and qualities of the Kamaras are made more manifest by other important and relevant considerations.

The fact that IAMTECH is evenly spread in most parts of the regions which are not the birth places of the proprietors and founders makes an important point. It is the cornerstone of diversification they are determined to cement. They want to emphasize that service to country and humanity should not be limited to one's region of origin but rather extend to every corner of the country. Such hospitality in offering services could even be rendered outside one's country.

This important fact brings us to the logic behind the locations of the other two learning centres. They are in the Bo and Kono districts in the Southern and Eastern provinces respectively. They are not located in the northern region the birth place of Paul and Paula.

The Lunsar Centre offers relevant skills which could be utilized in the mining industry of the region. It also minimizes the hazards, difficulties, and challenges associated with travelling hundreds of miles in search of higher learning and marketable skills.

As with the other centres these considerations make the centre at Lunsar vitally beneficial for both IAMTECH and the township. These mutual benefits make the establishment of the provincial learning centres, including the one at Lunsar a vital source of national, socioeconomic development.

Unlike Kambia Rokupr and Lunsar in the north the two centres in Bo and Kono may not be that close to Guinea Conakry. Yet they are in provincial districts which are easily assessable by students from both Liberia and Guinea in the north, south and east of Sierra Leone's borders.

There is another symbolic significance about the presence and operation of IAMTECH in Kono. In addition to the social clout associated with it, it solves one significant social problem. This is the hub of Sierra Leone's mineral resources and national wealth. In years gone by, it was the breadbasket of the nation. The bulks of the massive and lucrative diamond extraction industries in Sierra Leone are found in this region.

There is another side of this massive wealth. Its disadvantageous social aspect has grossly undermined economic development in the past. Not all that glitters is gold and in fact diamonds are the curse, the very nemesis of the region and the country at large. The craze to amass quick and enormous wealth from mining diamonds, especially by the younger generation, has been counterproductive.

Prior to the advent of the 1991 civil war the dropout rates among young people was massive and alarming. Now that IAMTECH has set up an institution of higher learning and offers marketable skills, the numbers of those that drop out of school has been reduced drastically. When the senior management team of IAMTECH visited the Kono campus, they were excited to learn that most of the students openly confessed that the craze for the acquisition of quick wealth from diamonds was grossly misleading. It is a blessing in disguise that IAMTECH is now a concrete, reliable alternative to the diamond fields.

The benefits associated with the pursuits of skills and qualifications in this day and age cannot be overstated. They are long lasting and that they can hardly fail people. Hence the saying goes, learning is better than silver and gold.

The Bo campus, like her sister campuses in Freetown, Kambia and Rokupr has underscored one significant point. This college has made inroads into the suburban habitats of the nation as part and parcel of the regeneration of the social capital Sierra Leone urgently requires in this post-war period.

# 26

# Community Relations

One religious leader once said that our faith is rooted in service to the Maker as well as giving freely to the needy. The best character, attitude, and behaviour to emulate and put into practice is the act of giving freely. Of all the virtues people must practice at all costs is that of a cheerful giver. Giving freely is service to God Almighty and humanity.

Paul and Paula are faithful, prudent and ardent Roman Catholics. Service to the good Lord is their priority. I realized at once that we are all Roman Catholics. They serve God through fervent prayers and supporting people and community organizations.

When I honoured their first invitation as their guest in 2011, they lodged me in their premises in one of the secluded areas of down town Freetown, according to the American popular cliché.

They relish discussing meaningful subjects that are of real benefits to their communities and country. They keep abreast of daily events, including national and international affairs. They discuss education their passion and contemporary subjects which deal with problems as well as the potential strategies that will make their communities and country better.

The first time I visited them was during one of the college's convocation ceremonies. I spent only one week with them and then returned to London. The room in which they lodged me was typical of Catholic or religious homes. In one of the drawers beside my bed there were a Catholic Bible and a Book of Prayer. I felt at home at once being a Roman Catholic myself. It was during the Easter break so we celebrated the Catholic Easter rituals together at the St Anthony Church in Freetown.

My second visit was spectacular. I came in the capacity of the college's convocation public orator. I guess, and rightly so, that I handled the role ably. I had a handful of exciting, congratulatory messages for my successful performance. I am gratified to reveal and note with immense respect that one of those that I impressed was the distinguished Professor Taylor Pearce. He is a Pro Chancellor at Fourah Bay College, University of Sierra Leone.

Paul and Paula are not just worshippers or like those who attend mass once in a blue moon. They are committed Catholics. They support the church financially and morally. In addition to their regular dues, they finance some vital projects. It is no surprise that their names are inscribed on the plaques of some of the Catholic parishes for their generosity and fervent commitment. All the parishes compete to have them as their permanent parishioners.

For instance, they used to worship at the St Martins De Pores Parish where they rendered massive financial and moral support. When they moved to their home far away from the church, they had no choice but find another parish close to them. The only way they could escape the regular lunatic traffic jams in Freetown was to move over to the St Anthony Parish, just a stone's throw from their home.

How the priest and their fellow parishioners at St. Martins De Pores would have loved to retain them as one of theirs forever! Wherever husband and wife go they always leave strong impression with people which speak volumes in their favour. That is because they render service to God and community. The couples are dignified people whose giving spirit goes far beyond the perimeters of the church.

As the saying goes service to communities means service to God Almighty. I said earlier on that they also render service to their communities. In the communities, they visit orphanages and give alms to the poor and needy. Faith is also manifested by opening one's doors to the fatherless as well as homeless. They have adopted many children without parents thereby giving them a new lease of life. They educate the adoptees and make their lives functional and beneficial to themselves and society at large.

Curious to know the rationales behind their gifts and sacrifices to the Church and communities, I asked them some questions. I commented: "I know that you are practicing Catholics. However, I am extremely impressed by your generosity to the Church and society at large"

"My wife and I are committed without qualification to the Church and the needy for the good reasons for which the Lord created and empowered us."

Paula sustained the points made by her husband. "I don't think it is difficult to understand. My husband and I believe that a good and committed Christian is the giving one. Greed, selfishness, pride and arrogance have no place in the members of Christianity or Islam"

I said, "That reminds me"

"Spill it!" she urged me.

"No it is not different from the subject matter"

"That is why I am almost at pains to prevail on you to spill it Doctor," she reiterated.

"Well I mean to ask you whether this Christian belief of yours is the cornerstone of the motto of IANMTECH"

"Of course, we established this institution on the basis of our Christian faith and values. To be of service to humanity and country is one of the cardinal points of religion and faith"

"The religious implication of the motto is that by serving humanity and country, you are serving God"

Paula smiled and confirmed. "Precisely so, my dear, you have hit the nail on the head"

In addition to their own personal contributions, they also hold responsible positions in the Church and in the community. Their children also play responsible roles- for instance Paulina is an Altar girl in the Church. Like her parents, she and her brother Michael are learning from their parents, that to be of service to humanity and country, one has to serve God and be a cheerful giver.

# PART EIGHT

# 27

# Accolades

It is significant to note that in its two and a half decades of existence IAMTECH has won numerous awards. These awards have actually elevated IAMTECH to a new and enviable level. It has become a force to reckon with in the tertiary sector of post war Sierra Leone. In terms of the quality education and the relevance of the programmes the college offers, this new institution has held its own among the very best in the country, if not in the region.

The college has won awards as symbols of appreciation and in recognition of its academic success. Higher educational institutions should meet certain criteria to merit awards, such as relevance and quality of the courses on offer. Discipline, retention and good behaviour of students are also taken into account.

The college has lived up to the highest of expectations since it became a tertiary institution. Discipline as a solid rock has cemented the success stories of the college. Thankfully, these contributions have not gone unnoticed in the highest of political quarters. The president of the Republic has lent his honourable voice to the team of eminent personalities that have recognized the contributions of IAMTECH.

President Dr Ernest Bai Koroma is on record acknowledging the contributions of IAMTECH to national development through its relevant, productive courses. This awesome pronouncement was made by His Excellency when the senior management team visited State House, to offer their financial and moral support to combat the Ebola epidemic.

It should be noted that IAMTECH was not the only institution that joined the battalion of institutions in Sierra Leone that lent their support to the president, his government and the nation at large during the ravages of the Ebola epidemic. The University of Sierra Leone was among the big names that rendered their support. The act is symbolic of the national character of Sierra Leoneans we are closest and most supportive and more patriotic when we are hit by catastrophes.

One culture that has emerged of late in the post war period is the acknowledgement of quality and overall performances of educational institutions. The media makes a huge contribution by gracing it at important social venues, such as Miata Conference Centere, Bintumani Hotel Hall, among other big national social centeres.

IAMTECH is affiliated to reputable overseas awarding bodies. They are internationally recognized, accredited bodies and institutions which do not merely rubberstamp institutions. They equally award educational institutions on the basis of stringent guidelines and requirements, which the institutions or awardees must qualify for.

In the vital disciplines of petroleum, oil and gas, as already mentioned, the standards and accreditations body in England have granted IAMTECH awards because of its robust adherence to the laws by which all their institutions around the world should conduct themselves.

Oil, gas and petroleum courses have earned the college more accolades. To reiterate IAMTECH is the only institution that offers these courses up to degree level in Sierra Leone. The importance of these courses need not be emphasized. Sierra Leone is recovering from three national devastations the civil war, the Ebola epidemic and the recent floods.

There is also an important national economic dimension to the viability of these new courses. With the oil exploration in the Bonthe District, graduates of IAMTECH in oil, gas and petroleum stand the chance to be gainfully employed in the industries. They will also be well equipped to contribute their quotas to the government's agenda for national renewal and prosperity.

The institution is very ambitious and its ambition knows no bounds. This value is inculcated into students the moment they enrol. Students participate in various internship schemes from which they receive awards. The petroleum, oil and gas faculty offers such schemes on regular basis.

The faculty even goes further and conducts conferences and seminars based on practical mining sites sensitization programmes and their inherent hazards. During these internships students are taught how to tackle the challenges and hazards that workers face in these industries. Awards are given at the end of each of these functions.

It has now become a routine practice for students to go on visitation tours as part and parcel of the practical aspects of these courses. Awards are given to participants not only to motivate them but also to attract more entrants into the courses. This strategy actually helps to boost the enrolment drives for this and related disciplines.

The upcoming college should be proud of the accolades showered on it since its inception. These glittering feathers in IAMTECH's cap make the forthcoming celebrations of their Silver Jubilee all the more significant. The celebration will mark signs of grace and gratitude to all those who have contributed to the success stories which have made IAMTECH walk with shoulders high, like gallant, brave and victorious veterans.

# 28

# Overseas Imports

The quest for excellence is not new in the diversification and modernization plans and policies of IAMTECH. Excellence, diversification and modernization are not mere words or concepts. The college is driven by these words as the kernels of their aims and objects. They are key values that constitute IAMTECH. The authorities of the institution are also conscious of the fact that knowledge has wide impact and overcomes all the inherent barriers manifested in geopolitical and cultural differences.

But there is one fact we can't afford to run away from. We can't afford to conceal it and it would be a shame to do so. Holding on to the adage that we can't afford to hang out our dirty laundry is neither credible nor beneficial anymore for Sierra Leone. It is an open secret that the country is short of people with the right skills, qualifications and functional experiences.

This does not mean that Sierra Leoneans are by nature less intelligent. There are brilliant Sierra Leoneans whose expertise has made it possible to hold their own among the very best minds in the world. Despite all these facts, which have elevated Sierra Leonean nationals as among the best in the region and the African continent, if not in the world, the skills shortage continues to affect the country's standards and by implication its socioeconomic development. In reality, Sierra Leone is short of experts.

IAMTECH is aware of the existence of these very important vacuums. Hence it always brings experts from overseas to fill them. Above all the institute knows that the aptitudes of experts vary from one discipline to the other, so most of the imports are unique in their own right. They bring new breadth, weight and vitality to the ideal type of tertiary education that post war Sierra Leone urgently needs.

Also, it is ideal to visualize that importing overseas experts means sharing relevant skills and knowhow across a variety of disciplines. It also creates the opportunity for cross-curricular and interdisciplinary breeding.

In this exciting age of interdisciplinary studies and the mass movements everywhere of workforces, including experts as well as non-experts, exchange programmes of this nature are very necessary in educational institutions. They will improve and sustain quality and standards in education.

Before the outbreak of war socioeconomic and related problems had hit most countries in Africa. They suffered from the cliché, brain drain. Sierra Leone is one of the countries that became a victim of the brain drain.

Sierra Leone had a relatively good percentage of indigenous experts in the late 1950s and early 1960s. The country was so comfortably supplied that it had to export some of them to the Sub-Saharan region and the former West Indies.

In the succeeding years, lightning struck, and the country and others in Africa were hit by the brain drain virus. Entering the civil war period in 1991, the economy shrank further and poverty crept in. By then most of the experts had migrated to the neighbouring Republic of the Gambia, to Ghana and even to Europe and America. Throughout these times of turbulence and uncertainty in the system, the importation of foreign experts took central stage. Another factor also precipitated the importation of overseas experts the shortage of expert staff in the new disciplines that IAMTECH was keen to offer.

The relentless quests to be innovative and bring a breath of fresh air to the tertiary sector meant the institution was likely to be hit by the brain drain and lack of expertise. So it had no choice but to find ways and means of filling the vacuums. Importation of experts was the only feasible strategy that would resolve the problems.

There were two categories of these foreign imports. There were those who came on sabbatical leave, taught and left at the expiration of their vacation. Others flew in, gave lectures and conducted seminars, workshops, presentations and conferences and then returned home. Between 1998 and 2013, close to 8 percent of the lecturers that rendered services to IAMTECH in the three categories mentioned, apart from the indigenous staff, were overseas imports.

Consultants and renowned educational investors and other professionals were also part and parcel of the overseas imports that the college utilized successfully to boost its programmes over the years. For examples, overseas investors in education, especially in information technology and related disciplines, worked hand-in-hand with the college authorities in order to augment and enhance the existing programmes.

Regular seminars, symposiums and conferences are held at the main college campus in Kissy Dockyards, Freetown. At these activities these experts showcase their talents and the projects they have successfully undertaken in the past. The academic atmosphere and climate created by the experts and investors inspires both students and the institution's indigenous local staff and other interested people.

In addition to the regular importation of overseas experts, the institution sought professional advisers abroad as consultants. This version of the overseas imports was similar to the distance learning method discussed in a separate chapter.

Above all, such academic activities promote the profile of the institution and market it internationally. The college has its own website on which it markets and promotes itself, meaning that it is very conscious of the importance of advertising and marketing strategies in the business of education these days.

One commentator has said that the competitive nature associated with recruitment and admission in educational institutions has completely changed the manner in which authorities market their institutions and themselves. Pamphlets and radio and television advertisements are no longer enough to promote educational institutions. Authorities have to embark on international promotion activities in order to attract students as well as the most qualified lecturers.

The very physical presence of personnel imported to render service to institutions, whatever the service may be, arouses curiosity amongst students and staff. Human nature is driven by curiosity, with a cogent ambit of invention and adventurism.

The commentator cannot be more certain for we live in an age where presentations and appearances matter in whatever we may engage in. In fact, education needs more promotions and advertisements than any other business or commercial activity these days.

The importance of foreign experts, teachers and lecturers is nothing new in the field of education in Sierra Leone. There were the grand old days of the US Peace Corps and the British Voluntary Service Overseas. These countries sent their personnel to Africa, including Sierra Leone and elsewhere in the world to work in almost every facet of the institutions of these less developed countries. Their expertise ranged from teaching of various skills in primary and secondary schools to rural agricultural development and other related vocational enterprises.

The Peace Corps was conceived by President John F Kennedy. Britain's VSO performed similar tasks in an attempt to ease the skills shortage and sustain the gains made by the British during the colonial era. I asked Dr Abie Puala Kamara to comment freely on the overseas importation that IAMTECH has successfully employed to its advantage.

"I have no doubts in my mind that the programme has been of immense benefit. It has boosted our quality as well as added to gains our indigenous local staff have made over the years. But I want to believe also that it has brought mutual benefits to the two sides. One thing I should remind you of is that some of the importees are Sierra Leoneans resident overseas. You are one of them. I mean that the importees and the host institution have gained from one another. In fact it is a cultural exchange programme like the Peace Corps and VSO programmes in those days"

I was put on the spot, so I responded, "Of course I am one of them, and I think as you said it has been of mutual benefits to both parties.

"In your educative comments, you mentioned two other historic programmes. They are the US Peace Corps and the British VSO. Tell me more about them"

"Well anyone born in the 1950s and 60s must be aware of these two overseas voluntary groups. The US Peace Corps were everywhere in Africa, the Caribbean and many more places. They came on one or two year contracts to work in various areas of national development. They adapted easily in our rural communities, learned the local languages and spoke them fluently. They were also very efficient and hardworking personnel"

"And the VSOs were they also hardworking?"

"They, like the Peace Corps worked very hard. They were very efficient as well. Most of them were here to teach the English language in our schools. Others taught other subjects and helped in other key areas, including sanitation in rural communities"

"What else did they bring to Sierra Lone as foreign experts?"

"In addition to their various vocations, they were also intercultural ambassadors. They brought their cultures, including music, dress and skills firmly rooted in their cultures back home. As I said before, we gained from each other because they also took a lot away, including our culture, language, beliefs and traditions of our various ethnic groups. Some of them interacted socially and made long term friends. It came as no doubt that when they returned to their countries, they wrote books about our cultural practices and religions"

IAMTECH could be termed an international tertiary institution to a large extent by virtue of its international connections and collaborations with other recognized and reputable colleges and universities worldwide. This is not a new phenomenon as even in the advanced capitalist West, tertiary institutions and universities encourage the idea very much. The Institute of Education, London University refers to itself as a Global University. The same applies to the perceptions of countless others around the world vis-à-vis their international relations or intercollegial ideals and policies. Institutions are corporate bodies, and like human beings, they rely on social interactions and collaboration for their success in their aims and objectives.

This phenomenon underscores the fact that knowledge is a universal or global virtue that needs to be shared in that context. It is no surprise that IAMTECH has inculcated and practiced similar ideas and continues to celebrate them as rich culture. The programme is synonymous with a cultural exchange on a rich and beneficial scale.

This brand of education also reflects the celebrated norms and the values of the historic cultural exchange programmes which the United Nation's UNICEF heralds and financially supports around the world. It is glorified as one of the tangible strategies, a crossbreeding education strategy, aimed at building global bridges. Specifically, it promotes global peace and harmony and generates social benefits as well.

# 29

# Changing of the Guards

Throughout history, no manner of transition has been smooth. More often than not transitions of all types have faced resistance. While some transitions have been marred by divisions and intrigues, others have experienced minor hiccups and frustrations which often mar the essence and rationales of the transition project. However, by hook or by crook, by quick fixes or otherwise, through the turbulent process light appears at the end of the tunnels and illuminates the entire process.

Here at IAMTECH many significant events took place prior to the changing of the guards. Among others, the founders had administered the college successfully for two and a half decades all by themselves. Against the odds, a catalyst emerged by leap of faith. At that time in 2010, the institution carved an affiliation bond with Njala University. It is instructive to note that the affiliation with Njala University is actually a saving grace for IAMTECH.

Prior to the forging of the historic relationship with Njala, a wave of turbulences crept in and threatened to rock what had been a relatively steady boat. To reiterate, through grace and leap of faith, the administrators of IAMTECH, with their faithful sympathizers and friends pulled through successfully and Njala and IAMTECH became twin partners by mutual consent.

So one would ask- why did they want to withdraw from the field? There are many answers to be borne out of that question. However, a commonsense answer would suggest that they wanted a breath of fresh air by taking a backseat.

Dr Mrs Lauretta Will-Sillah studied in the United States of America. She holds a doctorate degree with years of successful lectureship experience in distance learning under her belt. Inspired by patriotism, she and her husband, a politician decided to come and serve their country.

Towards the end of April in 2014, the author of this book had a successful training workshop. It was called the Vision Workshop 2014. The selection of venue was as beautiful, sensible and inspiring as the aims and objectives of the workshop. The venue was by the beachside in Freetown. The sea breeze was soothing and very inspiring for a terrain where the sun shines for almost three quarters of the year.

We didn't have to break a sweat, nor did we need electrical or locally made fans to keep us cool. We had cool and fresh air from the beautiful Atlantic Ocean in abundance. The food was delicious too and the free and interaction between staff was superb. It was a glorious atmosphere as if the world might turn out to be like that forever. At one point, reflecting on the scenery I told myself how saintly, how marvellous!

By then Dr Mrs Will-Sillah had officially taken her new, enviable seat as the principal of the institution.

Little did we know that like the rest of the nation, we were all drowsing in a fairy tale! Sadly months after that historical, wisdom seeking workshop, the Ebola virus struck in Sierra Leone. It coincided with Dr Mrs Will-Sillah's holiday to the United States.

After it was clear that the virus was abating, she and I returned to base at IAMTECH. My arrival coincided with the convocation in May 2015 by then schools had begun reopening and the state of affairs was normalized.

The convocation was succeeded by what will go down in the history of the institution as an historic meeting between the founders and proprietors and the senior management team. It was held at the Sierra Leone Teachers Union Hotel venue in Freetown. The modalities of the official transition from the old management (proprietors and founders) to a new one was discussed for hours and concrete decisions were taken signalling the birth of a new era on that memorable, historic day.

It was followed by another meeting between the new management, the founders and the entire staff. This time it was held in the Staff Commons in the main campus building. The founders announced that they had handed over to a new management team. The new management team that was constituted comprised the principal Dr Mrs Lauretta Will-Sillah Professor

Patrick Unisa Taylor, the Vice Principal Academic Affairs Dr Michael N Wundah, the author of this book as Vice Principal Administration and the former college Registrar, Rev Fr Dr Victor Summah.

It is unfortunate that Rev Fr Dr Victor Summah left the college towards the end of the second semester close to the receding of the Ebola epidemic in the country. He is a fine gentleman with huge potentials he could exploit successfully wherever he chooses to work as an academic, in addition to his vocation as a Catholic priest.

The transition brings us to the crucial issue of the implication of the usage of the phrases "new management" and "changing of the guard" "The adjective *"new"* when added to a common noun like *"management"* often creates ripples. "As for *changing of the guards*" it even runs into series of complex interpretations and connotations. More often than not it creates misgivings, misunderstanding and even scepticisms either by design or by default.

Anyway, leaving behind semantics in the interest of time, Paul and Paula did hang up their boots in the presence of the entire staff on that day. The new guards have emerged since that announcement was made by the old guards. That being said, contrary to any doubt, the advent of a new management in transition at IAMTECH was set to defy the traditional logic. As time went by, all hands were gradually on deck and things began to happen. As expected the team went to work straight away. Reforms were planned sustained by frequent meeting of management as well as general staff. The intention was to inject and sustain trust. It was a well-planned charm offensive which often bears fruits in the world of management.

I must confess that sometimes the early period of the transition was greeted by scepticism on both sides of the old and new complexities of the team. We were not surprised at the misgivings and premonitions we all shared or harboured against one another.

This is why. Change of any kind has its inherent complex anticipations, aspirations and mixed results. Therefore it is not wrong to state that change could be interpreted as hope for the future as well as despairs that might creep in unexpectedly or otherwise.

In this case, the early hours of the transition promised hope as well as everything being at stake from a pessimistic point of view, there were obviously those on the fence about the transition. One can't blame these people. Critics may call them the undecided or whatever name suits the make-up of their psyches that led them to feel or react the way they did. Let us put things in perspective. These staff had been literally yoked to the old management team for years.

An estimated three quarters of the teaching staff had attended IAMTECH as students, graduated and then become lecturers after acquiring further qualification in Sierra Leone or abroad. They had accepted the proprietors and founders as their role models, godfather and godmother. Hence it wasn't going to be that easy to break away and join a new management group they hardly knew. Together with their colleagues and founders, they had built amazing success stories with the little resources at their disposals.

There are individual differences in situations such as the ones we faced during the initial stages of the transition and it is inevitable that these human differences would come to the fore. Tensions were high as some people's emotions ran high in the room on that day. The future of the institution was up in the air and could not be easily predicted, not even by soothsayers. Apparently our collective fates, both of the institution and the human beings involved were in the hands of the gods!

# 30

# Building Rome

"We were somehow new to the old guards. And as they say, mindsets vary. Conscious of the facts we were constrained to remember at all times that we were total strangers in their midst. Some of them did also realize that some hearts inside them were bleeding inside as if they were bereft of their loved ones"

That was scribbled down in my personal notes after months of reflection.

One of the reminiscences that came almost with watered eyes, compounded with voice of sorrow, uttered silently, *It is not easy to part with someone you've known since you were a teenager.* 'The two quotations come from imaginations but they can't be separated from the human instincts and feelings in situations such as the ones I am describing. In that room, on that hectic day, there were humans with emotions and so their thoughts and feelings could not be much different from the two quotations above and the one below.

Of course, the newly appointed principal, Dr Mrs Lauretta Will-Sillah knew that Rome was not built in a day. It would surely take time for all to sink in. The handing over ceremony was not necessarily accompanied by pomp and pageant but it was solemn by virtue of its inherent logic and future implications for all and sundry.

The entire staff assembled in front of us. Some sat like Dagon before the Ark of the Covenant. At one point we could picture them and how they felt inside as we sat at the high table. Others sat like school pupils in front of a dictatorial head teacher and his vice and senior teachers.

Then suddenly one voice emerged. It was faint but audible, because the room was quiet. The voice said the following in one single, simple sentence."We are finished"

And then one senior lecturer sitting next to a junior colleague that was weeping made a frantic attempt to console him. In fact the comforter or consoler couldn't bear it himself burst into tears.

He uttered these two long sentences: "We have taken Mr and Mrs Kamara as our parents. Parting in the name of a new management regime from the United States and United Kingdom is not going to be an easy thing for us. Our hearts and theirs have been tied together for over two decades"

There was another distraught lecturer, he too was in tears. I heard his trembling voice say in sorrow, "We can't easily transfer our loyal, steadfast hearts to anyone"

I have to confess that it was on that historic day in the history of IAMTECH that I realized how diplomatic the founders are. Not only that, one could feel the spirit in the room, the atmosphere that was created by their ever loyal and committed staff.

Considering all the thick emotional outpourings, the founders handled the session very well. By the time they had made the necessary announcements and some key clarifications, there was an apparent normalcy. There was now palpable sense of hope, security and the prospects of a brighter future. Miraculously, the fresh feelings and an air of optimisms swept across the room as the meeting continued. At that juncture, it was now punctuated by spontaneous laughs. Why wouldn't they? Anyone could of course! They were now guaranteed a swift transition without any major hiccups by the founders, their benevolent employers and father and mother figures.

Pa Kamara and Mammy Kamara assured them in good faith: "My wife and I can't afford to tell you lies that there won't be hiccups in this period of transition. Surely it is only natural for there to be hiccups during the initial stages, but they will be short lived. There won't be any major ones that will derail the process and put anyone's future in jeopardy"

"With the passage of time we shall all grow in strength and get used to one another," said Mammy Kamara.

At this juncture we were elated. The negative perceptions held by the entire staff were completely dismissed by the founders. The hitherto grim faces indicating signs and feelings of frustrations and disappointment were miraculously transformed.

A little over thirty minutes after the meeting commenced the staff behaved as if they were hypnotized. They appeared in a jubilant and receptive mood. IAMTECH staff had indeed accepted the change of management, which they had apparently greeted with scepticism in their hearts!

Here the gist of a picture that was painted on that day by one of IAMTECH's heads of department (HOD) "To the philosophic mind that atmosphere was superficial to say the least. True acceptance of change of any nature should not be judged on the basis of sweet utterances and a party atmosphere. True change takes more than that. It is informed by change in the mindset, attitude, behaviour and character of the people that have been yoked to the old ways of doing things. Yes, the proprietors and founders have laid out in the open the challenges as well as the bountiful benefits this change in management might bring. He and his wife have admonished the staff in official tone as expected of them in the given circumstances"

Those comments or observations sound a bit to me like a note of caution. It sounds as if the HOD was one of those who had apparently decided to sit on the fence.

It is ideal to produce verbatim some parts of the keynote address of the founders.

Professor Dr Paul Kamara: "Today is a great day in the history of this great institution of ours. We are in transition from the old regime to a new one. We have to thank you all for your loyalty and dedication to the rapid development of IAMTECH"

He meticulously outlined the key changes that will be pursued by the new administration. "We have to dump all the old things, some of which were inordinate. They are unhelpful for good practice. I must state that we are all aware of the old tricks which we did practice. They must cease with immediate effect. We are now under a new administration so we must play by the rules of their game not ours anymore"

His wife Abie Paula Kamara supported every sentence of her husband's utterances. "We are now a new breed and therefore we must go by the new ideas the new people that have been put in charge are going to put in place as from today. I don't want a display of dual loyalty. It is negative and unhelpful for the ambitions of the change the new regime has brought for all our benefits"

It was the turn of the head of the new regime Dr Mrs Will-Sillah to make the acceptance speech. In summary, she made these crucial points: "On behalf of my two able vice principals, Professor Taylor and Dr Wundah, I want to share the goodwill intentions expressed by the proprietors and founders of this great institution! We are now operating under a fresh administration and we appeal to you all for your support. No divided loyalty will be tolerated by us. Cooperate with us in all our collective endeavours which are good for this institution and all of us"

Professor Taylor and I alluded to the ambitions of the new dispensation. At the heart of which, we did state categorically that compliance to rules, regulations and ethos of the institution must be given priority.

Prof Taylor admonished the staff as follows: "If we want the new management team to succeed, we must give them our support wholeheartedly. It is all about teamwork and nothing else. Therefore, I appeal to you to give us your undying support. Together, we shall succeed in making IAMTECH one of the greatest institutions of higher learning in the sub-region"

In conclusion, I added my voice. Buttressing what my colleagues or speakers before me had said, I said: "The speakers before me have said all that needs to be said on this occasion. They have made the salient points we need to work on in order to walk guardedly along the path to greater, accelerated success at IAMTECH. The lecturers and administrative staff of this institution have worked very hard to prepare and empower any student that successfully completes their course for gainful employment. We promise that with your support we are going to sustain those values"

The questions which followed the announcements and speeches by the new management team sounded a lot of promising notes. By the time the session was concluded, it became apparent that the doubts and misgivings hitherto held by the staff had given way to hope and inspiration. The discussions were frank and so they were convinced. Eventually, they were all energized to work harder in order to earn massive success for country and humanity.

# PART NINE

# 31

# Quality Assurance

This institution prides itself on maintaining quality assurance in order to prove the worthiness and credibility of the skills and qualifications students acquire. It is because it lays high premium on the maintenance of quality assurance that it has become a household name in the country.

Every institution has its own ethos, but the issue of guaranteeing quality is of importance for its survival and credibility. Quality assurance and quality audit constitutes the backbones of the well structured system at IAMTECH. The rules and regulations which govern its assurance are binding on staff as well as students. It is part and parcel of the contract of employment and one of the admission criteria for students.

Students are strictly warned during admission and matriculation sessions that they must abide by the quality rules. Prior to these sessions, applicants' undergo a strict vetting system. Their documents, including results, transcripts, certificates, and diplomas are audited carefully in order to ensure their authenticity.

Examinations procedures are also vetted thoroughly. Questions papers are treated with the utmost seriousness, severity and sincerity. They are subjected to scrutiny by the heads of departments, deans, the examinations controller and the Vice Principal Academic Affairs who heads the Examination Committee. This is a credible body that ascertains the viability of the grades and final results before they are published.

By virtue of the affiliation the institution has with Njala University, all the scripts are subject to second marking. These procedures may be considered too rigid and regimental, but the fact is that they give the results and the qualification students acquire from IAMTECH more credibility. Regarding scrutiny of examinations or assessments, quality assurance is guaranteed from the commencement of examinations. During examinations sessions, every paper is strictly invigilated by neutral invigilators in order to ensure quality assurance.

Since its inception, this institution has neither been accused, nor found guilty of examinations fraud. With the decline in standards, the media has become ever vigilant. Like sniffer dogs, some journalists always come up with contentious stories about the leakage of examination questions, and sometimes these stories could turn out to be unfounded.

Assessments are divided into cumulative, continuous and examinations. These are sustained by dissertations for degree courses and long term projects for certificates and diplomas. They are marked internally as well as externally. The internal examiners or subject masters supervise and mark the dissertations and then present them for external verification to Njala University and the other external verifiers overseas.

It is in the college's evaluations and assessments guidelines that finalists must defend their dissertations through oral presentations (viva). During these formal procedures, questions and answers based on the presentations are assessed. The sessions are strictly supervised by senior team members.

These are not one off procedures, limited to only examinations, dissertations and projects. The lecturers and assessors are even more scrupulous from the day students attend their first classes when college reopens. Attendance and class contributions, presentations, seminars and class works are all graded meticulously throughout the year.

IAMTECH is not only affiliated to Njala University, given the fact that it runs courses which are externally accredited and verified with the consultation of the authorities of course. For instance the oil gas and petroleum courses are accredited externally. The external verifiers from the United Kingdom visit the institution from time to time to carry out their verifications and quality audits.

Maximum penalties are meted out to defaulters and those who collude with them. There are no exceptions to the rules. Staff members are even dismissed when they are caught in any act of examinations fraud or mischief. To repeat, since IAMTECH was founded in 1991, neither lecturers nor students have been found guilty of examinations fraud.

Like the quality assurance procedures, quality audit and accreditation are ongoing procedures. Regular reviews are conducted by the various officials in order to ensure that the benchmarks which have been set are met. Also, course contents are reviewed from time to time. Hence it is necessary to conduct regular reviews in order to ensure quality standards, and the curricula contents of all the new programmes. The various heads of departments and deans ensure that all the action points are redressed properly.

Elaborating on the quality assurance and quality audit system at the institute, I encouraged three key figures to give their candid opinions. Dr Mrs Abie Puala Kamara, as well as Mr Lamin, the examinations controller and his able assistant, Mr Kabia made some salient points.

Dr Mrs Abie Paula Kamara: "IAMTECH has kept very clean records regarding the issues of quality assurance and quality audit. As you will appreciate they form the bedrocks of our importance and essence as an educational institution"

Mr Lamin: "The examinations office is the backbone of this institution. We can't afford to make the slightest mistake. Working according to the principles and ethics of this institution is our priority. We signed onto work here in order to uphold them at all cost"

The appraisal by Mr Kabia was no different. He and his team leader sang from the same hymn sheets, the rigid and professional manner in which quality is handled at all the centres of the institution. Mr Kabia: "I have spent a brief while in this office but I have learned a lot. The skills I have mastered are assets in my career and they are transferable. IAMTECH is a great institution, respected throughout the land because this office works incredibly hard in order to maintain the highest quality standards."

Finally the backbones of any educational institution are solidified by the viability of its quality assurance and quality audit procedures and policies. That this institution has held its own amongst the elite institutions is a huge manifestation of the credibility of the programmes and qualifications it offers. These qualities underscore the fact that it deserves an autonomous university status.

# 32

# New Landscape

I have chosen to reflect on the Petroleum, Gas and Oil Department for all its inherent rationales as well as the messages it emphasizes. The existence of this department is pertinent to some of the key ideals of the institution. It exists in order to inject innovations into tertiary education in post war Sierra Leone. The new innovations under discussion depict the new landscape which is bound to define the type of tertiary education that will enhance accelerated social and economic development.

Undoubtedly, it has successfully achieved this vital aim based on the physical evidences on the ground. One of which is, the department of mining, oil, petroleum and gas programme. The other tertiary institutions in the country are not running this programme. IAMTECH is the first to introduce it in this country and is the only institution doing it up to degree level. The advent and effects of the civil war have been characterized by theorists as both devastating and inspiring. It is inspiring because it has created meaningful awareness among the polity, social planners and the populace.

Educational institutions could fall into one of the several categories that are now aware that the functions of education have to change if the issues cited as the causes of the war are to be eradicated. This is an age of renaissance, which realities should be reflected in the programmes that educational institutions offer.

The social planners are equally aware that in view of the abundant national wealth, including mineral resources in the forms of diamonds and iron ore, Sierra Leone needs to redouble its efforts in economic development. Also, these mineral resources will not last forever. The economy needs to diversify only then will Sierra Leone be well placed to save for a rainy day. "Repair the roofs when it is dry" says the wisdom of the sage!

Mining, petroleum, oil and gas are mineral resources that will come to the aid of an economy that depends largely on diamonds and iron ore and of course, foreign aid for national development. By developing this department with the aid of government's subventions for students, it will boost the number of students enrolled on these productive courses. Without grants in aid for students the founders are doing their level best to continue running the courses which are already in high demand.

Considering the hurdles that the Institute of Advanced Management and Technology had to surmount in its early days of trials, it is correct to state that it has passed the tests of time. The rationales which constitute the inspirations of the founders also go a long way to tell us that they expected to find to find opportunities in the efforts and sacrifices they had embarked on.

I have to stress one salient fact for the benefit of readers. Opportunities are not gained or borne out of nothingness. They are borne out of innovations and innovative drives. Innovations are the enablers and drivers of human creativity, ambitions and determination. Over the years, this institute has been dreaming about the various ways it will continue to make a real difference in the tertiary sector. They reckon that this department is one of the dreams they wish to utilize for the benefit of posterity.

However, it is only prudent to address issues squarely creating the right balance when it comes to alluding to matters that involve the acquisition of knowledge. The programmes offered by the department are very demanding in terms of the learning and teaching resources.

It is fair to state that the available resources are relatively adequate for the number of students enrolled on the courses. These are attractive programmes which means that the potential for the department to grow is undoubtedly bright. IAMTECH is a private tertiary institution, which survives at the expense of only one means tuition fees, which in turn qualify the institution for grants-in-aid to deserving students. These go a long way to offset the expense required for the duration of their studies.

Without any government grants in aid the department will continue to knock its head against the wall to make ends meet. In the mean, the institution has applied several ideal strategies to fund the department. It publicizes the programmes through regular seminars, symposia, workshops and conferences. The dean of the department, Mr Sulayman Koroma and his colleagues are in constant touch with government ministries and other viable sources of revenues in both the private and state sectors. These are perceived as the potential ways of publicity in order to secure future funding and job prospects for successful students.

The economic prospects that these programmes have are huge. Therefore it is expedient that government demonstrates commitment to the diversification of the economy by funding programmes of this nature. Thankfully, the captain of the national ship has made a public pronouncement to the effect. President Dr Ernest Bai Koroma is on record as alluding to the programmes of IAMTECH as the providers of the rightful candidates that fill in 65 percent of the jobs in this country, in both the public and private sectors. He made this vital statement as an acknowledgement and approval of the ideals and educational functions of IAMTECH.

The management and academic staff at IAMTECH are happy that the president of the Republic of Sierra Leone Dr Koroma recognizes that courses such as the mining, petroleum oil and gas courses are the linchpins of the economic revival of this nation.

And the fact that he made this awesome pronouncement when the management, including the founders and principal made a courtesy call on him in the wake of the Ebola epidemic disaster is evident that he is aware of the existence of the vital, innovative programmes at IAMTECH, including the ones under discussion. The economies of the industrialized countries in the world may contract but have the ability to bounce back and serve the nation only due to the vitality and dynamisms of their educational systems.

The courses run by their institutions serve as the reservoirs for the consolidation and maximization of the yields of their economies. Sierra Leone has the opportunity to do likewise, provided the polity and social planners recognize and fund such programmes. No nation can afford to rely wholly and solely on foreign handouts otherwise it will continue to mortgage its autonomy as a sovereign nation.

Another strategy is the regular internships or job placements which have been mentioned elsewhere in this book. Through this strategy the college is well placed to kill two birds with one stone. How? Sending students on internships or job placing them in companies and industries or in mining sites creates the opportunities for job prospects.

The institution is equally advertised through these strategies, so as to maximize its enrolment figures. Potential investors may manifest interest in the department and the institution at large. Above all, it will create the climate for students to gain the necessary practical knowledge and vital experiences that will enhance their efficiencies in the vital areas of their future job choices.

# 33

# Autonomous University Status

I must open this chapter by making one important clarification. I have to do this due to its inherent significance. There is no written evidence to justify the claim that officials at the Tertiary Education Commission (TEC) are bent on refusing IAMTECH the status of an accredited autonomous university.

The only reason why such claims could be circulating is due to the sensitive nature of the very subject matter. Also as one would expect, the TEC is very secretive and conservative in nature. Those two adjectives are not meant to demean the ethos or characteristics of this important wing of Sierra Leone's educational system. Rather they are meant to underscore the honour and respectability it commands. Therefore, it is fair to state that the two adjectives are only meant to emphasize that the TEC is conducting itself in a well defined manner in order to maintain the honour, credibility and integrity of its status in the land as the certifier of tertiary and higher education status.

Hence in the absence of any freelance or commissioned announcements about the granting of university status to emerging or existing tertiary institutions in the land there will be wagging of tongues. This often results into claims and counter claims sometimes highly politicized and unfounded. Most important the quest by certain sectors of the popular press for regular changes of commissioners or directors at the TEC is not prudent. Considering the importance of the commission, stability is pertinent to its sustained efforts to make tertiary education work even better. We can't gamble and mortgage the stability and credibility of this all-important educational institution in the land. Such an institution should be filled with the finest minds of the land whose integrity is not in doubt.

In addition, when one takes into consideration the rich pedigrees and credentials and the lofty experiences of the chairman of the TEC, Emeritus Professor Kosonike Koso-Thomas Sierra Leoneans should conclude that the tertiary sector is in the good and safe hands of an internationally acclaimed academician.

Of course there are bound to be unfounded speculations, claims and counterclaims about the holders of such an enviable office. Therefore, it is not surprising that various opinions would be expressed. So let us do a summary examination of the guidelines which define the granting of university status by the TEC. Under normal circumstances, the definitions and criteria required for the accreditation of colleges to university status are straightforward. They ensure that quality assurance through auditing and inspections of colleges defines the key yardsticks which must be met by applicants.

The remarks by one Sierra Leonean educationist in the Diaspora, who had served in senior capacity at the Ministry of Education Science and Technology (MEST), truly underscore my point. He emphasized among other things: "I would like to observe that the criteria for measuring the standards of educational institutions for the validation of their accreditation should include assessment and evaluation. They should spell out the accreditation and the fulfilling of the stipulated entry criteria unto courses. "The latter requirements may be set by the country's Ministry of Education Science and Technology or a particular institution charged with such responsibility"

That being said, the fact is that rules and practices vary from country to country. In some countries, quality assurance and audit also have to do with issues of retention. That is a comparative study of the percentage of students who enrol and either complete courses or dropout for various reasons. It could also stray into pertinent areas like progression by which I mean securing gainful employment or progressing on to other educational institutions, including postgraduate courses.

Apply caution to the phrase "under normal circumstances". By that I simply mean to say all being equal, then quality assurance and audit practices are not normative or optional but goals requiring compliance to justify accreditation.

However, considering the change in political and social climate, which has more often than not impacted on provisions, *under normal circumstance* has become a buzzword, a political cliché. It has assumed contentious conceptual interpretations and the meaning varies from one climate of provision and accreditation to another. To most people it is like a political cliché, to others it is the yardstick which epitomizes life and death, an imperative often found in the ledgers or diaries of inspectors of educational institutions.

In the Western industrial countries, including Great Britain, the jobs of inspection regimes are fairly straightforward. Quality performance or audit is one of the main boxes, the imperative criteria which institutions must tick, before the inspectors pronounce them certified to provide education. The possibility that inspectors will sign off the quality portfolio of institutions is predicated on meeting the minimum requirements as stipulated by the quality control commission. The name of this all-important institution varies from country-to-country.

Surely this is not rocket science but there is a catch 22 scenario. It is a rather an unusual, unnatural headache associated with the interpretation and the viability of what actually counts as quality provisions and qualifications of educational institutions in the world of academia.

The idealists and their allies, the liberals would argue that the validity or viability of what counts as quality in most quality assurance and audit frameworks is very subjective. What counts as quality for one inspector of colleges or schools and related institutions may not necessarily count as such in the estimation of another inspectorate who may class the provisions or all of the items on the list as substandard.

In a very mucky political climate, the yardsticks for accreditation measurements are not as linear as they look on paper. This benign factor underpins the subjectivity of the concept under which rubrics inspection regimes operate, especially in amorphous states in most of Africa. Again, so the buzz phrase *"under normal circumstances"* is extremely contentious.

Sierra Leone is neither an exception to this bizarre inordinate happening, nor is it a peculiar case. Just across the Atlantic Ocean, in the other neighbouring countries in the region, such as Nigeria, Ghana, and their sister cohorts, qualifications for accreditation are subject to a lot of subjective rules, connotations and interpretations.

More often than not, these subjective barriers which have often hampered the chances of genuine, progressive educational institutions are borne out of the whims and caprices of some gullible and vindictive people at the top. In view of this reality, one can argue convincingly that the case of IAMTECH has not been necessarily constrained by it. This is a burning issue and it is ideal that we reserve it for another day!

IAMTECH is a quality driven tertiary educational institution. It operates on the basis of statutory regulations as stipulated by the laws of Sierra Leone, espoused and enforced by a statutory regulatory body. That body is known as the Tertiary Education Commission (TEC) based in the capital city, Freetown.

The versatility of IAMTECH underscores its international connections and relationships. In addition to the accreditation by the TEC, the institute is formally registered by other internationally acclaimed professional bodies and further and higher educational institutions.

These recognitions suggest one important reality. It is ideal for education, especially the tertiary tier to command global stature so that the viability of its qualifications, including certificates, diplomas and degrees is deemed certified internationally.

For obvious reasons, which are sometimes contentious, advanced countries like the United Kingdom, in particular, are known for their dismissal of qualifications from other countries, especially those in the Third World or less developed countries. Registering membership with external bodies, such as the Royal Society of Arts (RSA, ACCA, et al) adds pedigree to the educational status of their allies and associate members

It is the case, and a legitimate one at that that some people would look outside their immediate situation for greener pastures. Therefore they may consider it necessary to study and obtain qualifications beyond the shores of Sierra Leone and other less developed countries. It makes a sensible goal to study and gain qualifications with foreign names and academic seals of approval.

It is in this context that IAMTECH has registered with reputable international professional bodies as well as educational institutions outside

Sierra Leone. This is a bold and wise move by the proprietors of IAMTECH. Products of IAMTECH have gained admission to universities in the United Kingdom, the USA and elsewhere in the industrialized nations.

This move to create alliance with external institutions and undertake collaborative education programmes with them should not be misconstrued. It is not in the slightest measure a cheap attempt by IAMTECH to bend the rules and either distort or to undermine quality assurance at home or generally speaking.

There are strict membership guidelines which members are required to abide by otherwise the parent bodies abroad have the right to suspend or cancel the membership of associates or affiliates. Hence, IAMTECH adheres strictly to these criteria and policies of the quality assurance audits commissions of the parent bodies as well as the local ones in Sierra Leone, such as the TEC and Njala University. They all have strict guidelines which the college has always adhered to.

Of course all associations whether in the corporate world or academia have their rules which govern members as well as the advantages to which they are entitled. There are advantages associated with this international partnership. It gives international influences and credibility to their qualifications both internally and externally. Clearly it means that the graduates of IAMTECH are qualified and therefore they have the opportunity to gain admission into foreign higher educational institutions without impediments. Not only are there a lot more advantages but with the quality and recognition accompanying the membership procedures the products of IAMTECH also have the opportunity to attract employers.

Most graduates of IAMTECH have had admission to study abroad at prestigious universities. Recently a former IAMTECH graduate who served an internship at the college as IT lecturer and dean gained admission to one of China's prestigious universities to read computer science and technology at the postgraduate level.

The list of success stories is endless. Former students of IAMTECH have pursued postgraduate courses with flying colours in British, Canadian and US universities. Dr Sahr Gborie who works for the African Union (AU), was once an IAMTECH student and graduate. Scores of students have had such golden opportunities which they utilized profitably. These success stories have added more leverage to the reputation of IAMTECH as one of the most recognized, successful tertiary institutions in post war Sierra Leone.

# PART TEN

# 34

# Ebola Epidemic

The experts as well as the government have admitted that the nation was ill prepared for the outbreak of the Ebola virus in 2014. Even members of the international community, including the United Nation and World Health Organization and foreign governments were taken unawares by the rapidity and ravaging potentials of the virus.

In less than six months after the outbreak in 2014, the epidemic had destroyed lives and animals. It disrupted agriculture, the main sources of food and revenues for local famers, especially in the interior of Sierra Leone. In the cities and western area of the country, businesses and petty trading ventures were also affected seriously.

Education was hardest hit by the virus which developed into a full blown epidemic that swept across the country. The government had no choice but close down schools, colleges, universities and other learning outlets in the entire country. At first the government thought that declaring a public state of emergency would be misconstrued as igniting unnecessary panics among the population. However, when the number of nationwide deaths and quarantined per day increased beyond belief, the government had no choice but to impose a total ban. All forms of gatherings, trading activities, transportation and movements of people were prohibited under the umbrella of a blanket nationwide state of public emergency.

Strictures were enacted by the government. A state of emergency was declared due to what had now escalated into a full blown Ebola epidemic. The population restricted their movements as a sensible thing to do. Even at that, the causes of the Ebola virus baffled the population because even though all of these measures kept the population indoors, the numbers of casualties were on the increase daily.

Ebola is a baffling and mysterious virus because since the first outbreaks in the Congo, the proximate causes have remained problematic. Above all, diseases are put under control only when there are cures for them. Ebola is a peculiar case in this regard, as to this day no absolute cure has been discovered.

A paradox came with the ravages of the disease. Although it caused lasting, devastating chaos in Sierra Leone, still it reignited a national debate which had been swept under the carpet in easier times. In the end, the epidemic exposed the flaws of the health services in the affected countries.

The ambivalence and impunity of politicians in funding the strategic state institutions were unmasked. The lukewarm attitudes of the international community, including the UN, EU, WHO and most of the affected countries' international partners were revealed by the dramatic outbreak and impact of the disease.

Regarding the reactions of educational institutions, the thinkers, experts and education administrators and practitioners were pushed beyond their capability. They were made to think outside their small, limited boxes.

Towards the end of 2015 Ebola was officially declared over by the WHO and the government of Sierra Leone. Neighbouring Liberia was the first to have a clean bill of health, but few months later there were pockets of new Ebola cases. They were resolved quickly and the country was cleared once more. As of January thankfully, Sierra Leone has not reported any new cases, but government is still sounding notes of cautions.

In times of acute difficulties, history teaches that we need to think in the new ways reminding ourselves that survival of the fittest is the name of the game. The government and its subjects were meant to think seriously, critically and logically outside the box. People must try as much as possible to be creative too and work around problems thoughtfully and successfully.

And think outside the box, the government did, and to relatively successful effects. It adopted creative strategies beyond and above the imagination of most people. It was during the tail end of the academic year that the Ebola broke out. The Ministry of Education Science and Technology came up with a strategy to justify its relevance as one of the main stakeholders of education and skills in the land. It conducted school lessons for junior and senior secondary schools in the key subjects. Through this means the ministry kept the pupils busy as well as maintaining the hopes of the nation that steps were still been taken to gradually redress the problems.

Some may argue that the ministry's efforts were not equal to the impact of the devastation the thousands of lives the disease claimed and the rate at which it was continuing to spread in the country. However no matter how ordinary the efforts were through this particular strategy, education was now directly taken into the homes of pupils through radio lessons. Not that school lessons through radio and TV programmes were new schemes in the history of broadcasting in Sierra Leone. The old Sierra Leone Broadcasting Service (SLBS) used to conduct school lessons and other related programme decades before the outbreak of the virus. The difference between the two phases is that while the first phase was done for novelty's sake radio lessons were inaugurated during the Ebola outbreak out of necessity. Also, the authorities were able to make the vital political points that it was taking the necessary actions to keep the nation's hope alive and that they were not complacent as alleged by critics.

Despite all that the government and the educational institutions had a much more difficult problem to wrestle with. It was about finding meaningful solutions to the impact and disruption of the tertiary education programmes. Apparently, for almost a year and half, there was no answer in sight. The lingering aftermaths of the Ebola epidemic continued to expose the flaws and the limitations of most of the colleges and the constituent institutions of the University of Sierra Leone.

The ingenuity of IAMTECH was utilized to the full for the benefits of its students. When the Ebola outbreak occurred they were close to graduation season and students were writing their projects. The authorities had other ideas to at least minimize the wider ramifications, effects of the continuing class closures, lockdown and public emergency. Lecturers taught lessons through their distance learning programmes (DLPs) and mailed assignments and other related learning resources to their students throughout the land.

For every success story, there are masterminds. The mastermind for this successful scheme was the leader of the senior management team Professor PFE Taylor. He had been left to man the fort as acting principal. By then the titular principal, Dr Mrs Lauretta Will-Sillah was in the United States of America.

By the time she returned from the United States, Professor Taylor had taken positive actions. Backed by the founders and the team of hardworking deans and HODs they had galvanized all the resources and expertise of the lecturers. In the end, they prepared the students who had successfully completed their academic tasks, including examinations and projects for their convocation commencement ceremony.

The ceremony was held successfully in April 2015 to huge and glorious applause. By then, there were pockets of isolated cases mostly in some areas of the interior. The government and the key stakeholders continued to pursue the necessary drastic actions in order to combat Ebola once and for all. Sierra Leoneans had suffered the ravages of the Ebola epidemic for over one year. By the time the health experts realized that there were signs of drastic reductions in the number of cases and the death toll, arrangements were made for educational institutions to fully resume activities throughout the country.

Meanwhile structures were now in place to enhance the continued pragmatic actions of the government and Ministry of Education Science and Technology. To signify the importance of this breakthrough, all educational institutions were allowed to resume classes by May 2015. Above all the Sierra Leone government and her international partners and the stakeholders in the war against the Ebola epidemic were now given the confidence and assurance that all signs were indicative of the fact that light was beginning to emerge at the end of the tunnel.

I need to reiterate this vital point. The handling of the Ebola epidemic has mixed reviews which Sierra Leoneans and their government need to reflect on seriously. On one hand it did claim thousands of lives and seriously hampered the social and economic development of the nation. On the other hand, the paradox is that the epidemic put the authorities and their institutions under the microscopes. No more should Sierra Leoneans including those in authority be as complacent and ambivalent as they were prior the outbreak. By their own admission, they were caught unprepared. It goes a long way to urge the authorities to take concrete actions as they renew the shattered and dilapidated state institutions.

The government should forge a proactive partnership with the private sector and invest in training and research. The efforts of members of the international community, including WHO, UN and foreign governments have contributed immensely to the eradication of the Ebola epidemic. In the wake of their departure, they also left a reservoir of logistic support, knowhow and documentary resources for future detection, intervention, prevention and cure.

However, Sierra Leone needs to own the knowledge and the strategies their international partners utilized to combat the disease. How? Investment in education, training and research are the catalysts. We can only place ourselves strategically if we invest heavily in research and assign the right human resource personnel, talents and agents to the appropriate roles. When these necessary actions are taken, touch wood, Sierra Leone will be well prepared in case we are faced with such scenarios in future.

Higher educational institutions can't afford to run away from academic research ventures. It has been made abundantly clear that tertiary sector of our educational system should be a proactive partner in such endeavours. Proactive partnership in academic research is vital for the tertiary sector in order to justify their existence.

A future UNIMTECH is very much aware of this fact. It constitutes one of the uncompromising clauses of the contractual obligations of lecturers. In this period of transition to the acquisition of university status, there is an academic research journal in the pipeline at IAMTECH. It is intended to underpin the relevance of research to maximizing the speed of socioeconomic development.

# 35

# Convocation

The convocation ceremony at IAMTECH sums up the soigné of students at this noble institution. It is a special and memorable day in the lives of students and their supporters and loved ones in many respects. On this glorious and inspiring day, all those who supported the students during their studies, or struggle, according to their popular cliché, converge at the Abie Paula Kamara Amphitheatre.

The amphitheatre is situated in the institute's main campus, in Kissy Dockyards, Freetown. According to the customs and traditions of IAMTECH and her affiliate partners, Njala University, all convocations are held on the main campus of the institution. It is a day of pomp and pageant during which important dignitaries from all walks of life, including the Ministry of Education Science and Technology are invited.

Also, it is on this day that the realization actually dawns on the successful students that their dreams have come true at last. For the unfortunate ones, who fail to cross the River Jordan, so to speak, it is often a sad day for them. On this sad day they realize that they have been left behind in a race that might never come again. Hence they say opportunity comes but once.

One student, who couldn't graduate in May 2015, regretfully remarked in tears: "I might never come this close. In a family of six, I am the only sibling that has entered a tertiary institution. The rest of my siblings dropped out during their first and second years of primary and secondary schools respectively. And yet, when I had the chance to rewrite history for myself and our family, I too have flopped it."

They say success comes with loads of responsibilities. It comes with huge expectations. This is even truer in most underdeveloped as well as developing countries in the world.

In sharp contrast with rich developed countries, education is a right, not a privilege. It is a right as well as free, because they can afford it at the expense of the state and taxpayers' money.

In the United Kingdom, funding education has assumed the collective responsibilities of stakeholders. The module is known as public-private partnership. The public and private sectors fund education, especially tertiary education. The cultural implications for roles and expectations of parents and wards in developed and less developed countries are amazing. All the same the wider implications of university qualification are huge for the state, the graduates and their families, to say the least.

With qualifications, especially degrees, one is more likely to pay high taxes to the state than not. Moreover, education is a public good therefore those who pursue it are looked upon as assets, not liabilities. They have important roles in society as highly qualified and skilled individuals.

In wealthy countries, parents don't have to incur any debts in order to sponsor their children or relatives in schools, colleges and universities. So after graduation or certification, they don't have to pay back the debts they incurred in order to educate them.

The new arrangements in England and Wales stipulate that graduates are responsible for the student loans they incurred for their studies, not their parents. Even at that, they pay minimal amounts only when they secure well paid jobs. Therefore, it is optional for them to help their parents or not after graduation.

In poor countries, education is heavily financed by parents and wards. In extreme cases, parents sell off or mortgage their family property, including landed properties and plantations in order to pay school, college, or university fees. Hence, after graduation it is obvious that the financiers of the students are faced with payback time. Not only that, abject poverty may constrain only five in a hundred family household to graduate from college or university. It means that the five lucky ones are bound to assume the expensive roles of the breadwinners of Africa's extended family.

Factor all of these into the phenomenon. They will help you to envisage as to why the day one completes his or her course in Africa goes beyond an ordinary ceremony. It marks the beginning of assuming the role of a breadwinner for the immediate as well as extended families. Uncles, aunts, cousins, siblings, half-siblings and even step-parents become the responsibility of the new graduates.

All the same, the massive expenses that come with completing tertiary education in Africa, notwithstanding, it marks a memorable event in the life of any successful person. No one can afford to turn down the prospect of graduating from a tertiary institution. It is similar to a gem, which one can't afford to forgo, if given the opportunity to own one.

Here is a graphic eyewitness account of the colourful atmosphere of one of many IAMTECH's convocation ceremonies. "I was taken aback by the number of students that graduated on that occasion. I could not believe what I saw"

The eyewitness went on to describe the glittering, flamboyant occasion further: "By 9.30 in the morning all the dignitaries had arrived. The graduating or certification classes were already seated. The flowery single file group of academic staff, deans and head of departments all followed the marshal, who is the traditional, mace bearer of Njala University. By virtue of the affiliation with Njala University, their officials were there to perform the honours. The vice chancellor and principal of Njala conferred the degrees, diplomas and certificates on that day. The relics of the British customs and traditions have not only captured the imaginations of the former colonies. The traces are found in the rituals of the entire ceremony. On that colourful day as ever since the colonial era, the glittering and symbolic entails of the British universities were very much on display. The marshal or mace bearer of the convocation ceremony looked like a Victorian marshal, or the official who carries the floating regalia robes of the Queen during the state opening of the British Parliament"

Another eyewitness excitedly concurred as follows: "Their unique regalia and presence in those colourful marshal outfits do capture the attention of the audience. So was the marshal of Njala University, who officially doubled on the day for IAMTECH. The only difference between her and the British marshal or mace bearer is that though she carried the mace, she was not completely, impeccably clad in the peculiar British regalia outfits. However, she stood right in front of the long single file academicians who were clad in their academic robes and hoods. With the official mace in the hands of the marshal, her academic gown and the mace she carried crowned the pomp and pageant of this historic academic ceremony"

Another participant described the ceremony: "The group was accompanied by the officiating deputy vice chancellor of Njala University. On that occasion, the DVC was a female, the first ever in the University of Sierra Leone to hold such position. She stepped in officially on behalf of the vice chancellor and principal. She was immaculately robed, befitting her status. The procession was accompanied by the sweet, solemn melody of the Sierra Leone Police Band. As they filed past the excited crowd, one of them said in Sierra Leone Creole or parlance, 'Ah Papa God, Den say book learning sweet!" Meaning in English, it is indeed, sweet to be educated. With the national anthem played to thunderous applause, it was show time for the public orator and the acting vice chancellor and principal. The ceremony commenced and students were ushered onto the podium to receive their certificates, diplomas and degrees. It was a never-to-be-forgotten day in the life of the crowd of well wishers, wards and parents that came to grace this big day"

At any given convocation ceremony at IAMTECH, the numbers of graduating, certificating students have never been less than half a thousand. Even during the Ebola epidemic, whiles numbers dwindled or stalled in other institutions, the new entrants at IAMTECH increased unbelievably. Those who matriculated in May prior to the resumption of classes in 2015, the new admission class went up by a whopping six hundred students. The reasons behind the surge in the demographics of students have been highlighted in the preceding chapters.

The overall provisions and services of IAMTECH truly endear people to the institution. They are very much conscious of the fact that at the completions of their courses graduates are assured of securing jobs because their qualifications make them attractive to the job markets.

It is traditional for the authorities, preferably the vice chancellors or principals to make series of new announcements in their keynote addresses. At IAMTECH, their convocation is no exception. Long and short-term plans are announced on this very important day.

The 2015 May convocation was a case in point. The principal, who is doubling as the vice chancellor of a new autonomous private university in the making, spoke of short as well as long-term plans in her keynote address. Dr Mrs Lauretta Will-Sillah made an eloquent speech that touched the crowd. Every word, sentence, and paragraph of her speech was greeted by deafening, thunderous applause.

When she announced the preparedness of the institution to bid for an autonomous private university status, the amphitheatre erupted into a crescendo. The people had craved for this status for twenty-four years. Therefore, to break the news that they would soon receive it was more than exciting and joyous news for the audience to behold.

The good news was greeted with an excited comment in the audience. One member of the audience said: "The good times are finally here. The Lord has decided to finally give us a university of our own. The Kamara family will surely go down in history as the founders and proprietors of the first autonomous private unversity in Sierra Leone"

One disappointed person in the audence was in tears. Her daughter didn't make the grade, so she didn't graduate on that ocassion. She was in tears as she commented: "I wish my daughter was among this lucky, graduating class. They have not only become graduates of this noble institution, it will be recorded in history that it was on their convocation day that we were told that the long waiting will be over one day"

The ceremony was concluded by the tune of the Sierra Leone national anthem. The procession left on the dispersal tune of the Sierra Leone Police Band. They marched out of the arena in the order in which they entered it.

There was even greater and louder applause. IAMTECH have enjoyed many successful and flamboyant convocation ceremonies, but the one that was held in May 2015 was a ceremony never to be forgotten in the history of the institution.

# 36

# What the Future Holds

Interview anyone who runs a private college that is affiliated to one of the universities in the country, and they will reveal one thing. Their ambition is to gain university status and be autonomous. Even those that are not affiliated to any university entertain such ambition. I have said in passing elsewhere that human nature instinctively craves for liberty. The love of liberty inspired nationalist movements in former colonies in Africa, the former West Indies and the Indian subcontinent. Autonomy or sovereignty, they say is priceless. Besides, the situation in Sierra Leone makes this dream and ambition extremely pertinent. It is one of the catalysts for national development. People often say that Sierra Leone does not need to reach the population of Nigeria or Ghana in order to have three or more universities.

The need to diversify, to have more universities is driven by one fact. Not that Sierra Leoneans are not intelligent of course they are but it is common knowledge that the country is lacking seriously in relevant, viable skills such as those I have mentioned in the other chapters. And the logic is that the country needs to diversify and increase the chances of filling the skill vacuums. To enhance accelerated socioeconomic development, the skills banks have to be replenished, the more so now that the country is suffering from the hangovers of the brain drains even before the civil war.

The fact that the country keeps importing and hiring so-called foreign experts, consultants to help in strategic developmental areas justifies the claims I have made. Like it or not, the importation of foreign specialists and experts to help plan the Week of Education 2015 sustains this point among other things.

I am not implying that Sierra Leoneans and their government should shut the door to other nationals. We are a receptive nation that prides itself on international cooperation. Above all we live in the age of globalization and post-modernity, which means that all nations have been shrunk to a global village. We must share everything including cultural capital.

The shortage areas are in vocational skills. And this is not peculiar to Sierra Leone. Most African countries suffer from the same skills shortage in key vocational subjects. IAMTECH has always embraced and practiced the technical and vocational model of higher education, knowing the wider benefits it brings. They are still optimistic that the promised-land will be within their grasp one day. When this dream is realized, it promises not only university autonomy, it will give the institute an even more influential profile.

Acquiring this status is everyone's dream at the college. The staff members are determined to succeed which is why they work round the clock. It is a hot topic among both lecturers and students. One of the deans summed up the moods of his colleagues when he said, "IAMTECH is now in a euphoric mood. We are all excited by the prospects of teaching under the emblem of a university status. We can't give up because we are sure that once we meet all the criteria set by the TEC they will grant us autonomous university status. Our relentless support must be put to work in order to achieve this grand goal"

The acquisition of autonomous university status entails herculean tasks to say the least. Between 1994 and 2012 IAMTECH presented several applications and all the necessary documents for the attainment of the status. The affiliation to Njala University had lasted for over four years so the institution thought it fit to bid for an autonomous university status.

There are immense benefits associated with autonomy. Like a colonial entity that fought tooth and nail for emancipation from their colonizers and was liberated, IAMTECH has found itself in a similar situation. Freedom surpasses everything else one would wish for in life. Freedom fighters used to say that the struggle for independence was for the gratification of posterity. This is the ambition that galvanized and n-spirited the resolve and determination of the nationalists. They would settle for nothing less than autonomy. In a similar vein the lecturers and staffs at IAMTECH cannot afford to settle for anything short of university status.

The future University of Management and Technology acronym UNIMTECH) is a national project in the imaginations and consciousness of the aspirants. The proprietors and students are supported by a cross section of the Sierra Leone community. The concept and rationale is captured in this short paragraph: "It is meant to build the capacity of citizens of Sierra Leone and those from elsewhere to meet the emerging challenges happening beyond their shores. It will impact on the communities the college has served fruitfully all these years"

The paragraph goes on to the rationale into the following defined goals and objectives:

i. Quality Assurance

Quality assurance constitutes the backbone of any quality educational institution. The current students enrolled on its courses and those it later develops shall be well equipped with the necessary skills, qualifications and all the other relevant attributes for futures leadership.

ii. Viable Outreach Strategies

A future university shall reach out to every doorsteps of the communities in Sierra Leone. Currently IAMTECH has outreach courses in the form of distance learning, through which it teaches marketable skills. Over the years those who have acquired qualifications through distance learning have secured well-paid jobs in the private and public sectors of our country. Given the opportunity, when IAMTECH attains university status, it will be an asset in our communities. These achievements will even be maximized when it becomes a university. Local centres of learning will enjoy the benefits of university status because courses will be brought into communities closer to the doorsteps of consumers or students in remote areas where it has established learning centres.

iii. Convenience-Oriented Provisions

Adapting education to the needs of consumers or students requires flexibility. Timetables should be planned in such a manner that the hours when staff and lecturers may be contacted are convenient for students, especially mature students, who are often engaged in other important activities including part-time jobs. The timetables of their classes, projects, examinations and seminars will be organized to suit their personal circumstances. They will be able to reconcile their academic work and the demands of their jobs and family commitments. In other words, classes will be tailored to meet the needs of students.

## iv. Economy

In modern times, one of the criteria of an ideal type education that most people, especially the poor and disaffected prefer education they can afford. Especially, in the African context, a future university must focus on creating the necessary conditions for greater access to education. This strategy will minimize the dropout rates that have marred the system over the years. Reasonable fees will be charged in order to increase the level of enrolment. However this does not mean that quality will be compromised, because it is the key factor that the management has prioritized since the establishment of IAMTECH.

## v. Discipline

At the heart of the above criteria which constitute the aims and objectives of the future UNIMTECH, is discipline. The Protestant ethics is of primary importance in ensuring that no stones are left unturned in enforcing discipline at the future UNIMTECH. Discipline, we do believe is one of the pillars on which a formidable and productive society is built. History attests that all successful societies or nations have owed their success to disciplined attitudes and characteristics. Discipline instils the values of respect for law and order and for humanity and property. It is therapeutic for humankind and enhances social cohesion, which post war Sierra Leones needs more than ever before.

It is the middle management capacity building of the nation that the future university will put at the forefront of its priorities as it has done since the creation of IAMTECH. Strong community relationships are vital and necessary for the success of the university.

IAMTECH's success stories tell amazing tales. For instance, very close to its heart are the solutions of the many socioeconomic and psychosocial problems of the socially disaffected population of Sierra Leone. IAMTECH is known for lifting the poor and disaffected market women and farmers in difficult communities out of poverty and giving them life chances.

The college cares about the lingering gender disparity which has endured in our society for too long. It is pathetic to note that since independence gender discrimination has been one of social problems that successive governments and policy designers have not tackled. To date most of those who occupy top positions in our state institutions are men. This patriarchal social malaise has affected the social and economic development of Sierra Leone.

Not only that it has degraded the confidence and aspirations of most women who have paradoxically come to support the ideas and ideals of the patriarchal world and the myths around it. The myths sustain and promote the idea of a male dominated world and the superficial belief that women are inferior to men. Through this naked gender inequality and discrimination, quality has been grossly undermined and hindered. The resultant effect is that frustration has grown among those women who are cheated and disadvantaged due to their gender.

A future university in my estimation will be determined to empower women equally with men as IAMTECH is doing already. Especially, it will inspire and motivate those women who have suffered gender discrimination, so that they will be in position to dispel the myth that has imprisoned the innate ability of those who have been hurt the most.

It is gratifying to note that the offshoot future university that IAMTECH has in mind is the holistic type in its approach to educating multitudes across the nation. That is it will be all embracing and take account of students' social, economic, mental, physical and psychological conditions. An all-round educational provision has in view the learners as whole people. In a world fraught with complex challenges, curriculum contents and pedagogies should address the psychosocial and well as social needs of learners.

The senior management and all the experts associated with this institution are in tune with the desires and wishes of the consumers of their products. All the data relating to these vital matters suggest that they have spoken eloquently in favour of enhancing and sustaining the quality of teaching as well as the offering of programmes which have the potentials to attract lucrative jobs in the competitive job markets of the twenty-first century.

The current IAMTECH is a family, and so is the future UNIMTECH. It means that the entire staff and all who take part in the institution are there for one another. It is a brotherhood and sisterhood and is fervently holistic. As one family, the future university will jealously guide, preserve and cement the values which make the enterprise meaningful and beneficial for all the membership. This belief and its implications apply to how the management treats students and the communities it serves.

Like the current IAMTECH, its offshoot the future UNIMTECH will equally become a family and assumes the values that define such a union. It will be a compact unit, one homogeneous whole with its inherent diversities. As a mark of recognition for this perceived nature and characteristics, I decided to gauge the opinions of one of the many key players of the institution.

He is Mr Stephen Lamin, the examinations controller. He occupies this major position as well as being one of the longest serving members of staff. He also teaches one of the modules of the postgraduate course. "I have enormous hope for a successful future University of Management and Technology. It will be capable of enhancing massive success in the areas of nation building through character moulding of the students that pass through its doors successfully"

I asked Mr Lamin to reflect on the important area of discipline when IAMTECH becomes a university.

"I don't think our future university shall have any problem with discipline both among staff and students. Mind you we have never had a history of indiscipline at IAMTECH. We shall be the same when we become a university. Discipline is the cornerstone of a well refined person, and that is what education at this institution teaches both staff and lecturers"

Alhaji Abu Bakar was IAMTECH's acting registrar at the time of this interview. I asked him to comment on its viability. In his capacity as the acting registrar, he deserved the honour to comment on the institution. Besides, he has served the institution with distinction in many roles.

"It is an opportunity that we are on the verge of transiting into an autonomous university. The challenges are our responsibility to tackle. The onus is upon us to prove our mettle as a future university. I must confess that I have no doubt in my mind that we shall make this great nation of ours, Sierra Leone extremely proud of us for attaining such an awesome status. We shall work very hard, redoubling our efforts in order to meet the criteria set by the TEC. The founders and staff are quite aware that the TEC does not loathe us they are simply doing the right thing and as professionals, we do understand and we respect their decisions"

# 37

# Quantum Leap 1

The establishment of the current postgraduate courses at the Circular Road Centre is not only an innovative success story, it is a quantum leap. Not that there are no postgraduate courses in the higher educational institutions in the country. Of course there are, considering the fact that Sierra Leone had its first university in 1827.

The differences between the many postgraduate courses offered by the other sister institutions and the ones offered at IAMTECH are unique. IAMTECH's model is job oriented. The main objective is not only to augment the strengths and viability of the current skills or courses that are taught but to fill in the gaps and bring in other ideas in order to enhance their marketability.

Innovation and the drive to reach the unreachable together underlie the thinking that brought about the postgraduate programmes. The courses are capable of benefiting others no matter where they are. Generally speaking, it is the marketable values of the courses that have made them attractive to students. Every success story has a name or names associated with it. The names or contributors could be mentors, founders, proprietors or authors.

In the case of the postgraduate programmes at IAMTECH, the key architect behind them is Dr Mrs Abie Paula Kamara. Of course as always, her husband played a major role. They complement each other's efforts, which is why they have made a very successful team.

The Circular Road Centre is strategically located in downtown Freetown and is easily accessible. It may be reached from all angles of the city. The programmes attract students from all walks of life and were approved under the affiliation arrangements and protocols which bind IAMTECH and Njala University.

As with all the programmes offered at the other centres of IAMTECH, people were very much excited by the introduction of the Circular Road

Centre. It started with healthy figures. A lot of students enrolled on all the courses. By the time it celebrated its first anniversary, the number had increased to almost three figures.

The teaching staff is incredible. In addition to their enviable qualifications, they are a committed and dedicated team of experienced professionals.

The Circular Road Centre is very important apart from the leverage it gives IAMTECH. It is an inspiration to the entire institution.

---

The programmes are professionally driven meaning they earn students the right kinds of skills for professional jobs. The staff members who teach the courses are drawn from various professional bodies and other universities in addition to those staff at IAMTECH.

The programmes were expanded in 2015, incorporating the degrees of Master of Science in development/economics and the Master of Science in accounting and finance. The postgraduate diploma in education was converted into a master's programme.

There is a profound symbolism associated with the establishment of the postgraduate courses not least that it enhances the pedigree of IAMTECH in its aspiration to become a future University of Management and Technology. Above all, it reaffirms the philosophy of the institution and its founders. The kernel of that philosophy is that education is a public good and therefore should be made to serve everyone in society.

Greater access to all courses under the umbrella of diversification will be supported and funded by stakeholders. It is only when these conditions are fulfilled that the essence of education will become the public good we deem it to be. Circular Road in the heart of Freetown puts the rationale for locating the course in this particular part of Freetown to the test.

The current IAMTECH is not the only private tertiary provider. The beauty about the perceptions of the masses about the need to acquire education at this level is that the rush by almost everyone to gain one qualification or the other has become a national quest with a difference. The difference between this quest and others is similar to the history of revolutions and religious crusades. As those two enterprises were conducted through threats and duress, this particular quest is intellectual and does not involve any use of force.

The growth in the number of students enrolling on tertiary education courses is amazing in fact, it beggars belief! Government policy stipulates that greater access to education, through increase in enrolments in educational institutions is mandatory. Successive regimes have encouraged the populace to motivate their children to study up to the highest level. Hence, the surge in the number of students is not through competition, it is entirely voluntary.

One board member concurred: "The surge in ambitions to read up to master's degree among Sierra Leoneans is inspired by many factors. In addition to the fact that there are many Sierra Leoneans with first degrees among the educated, the ambition to read up that level, comes from the heart, not through threat or duress"

I would add that the job market has become extremely competitive and so applicants for jobs have no choice but to read further beyond first degree level.

The courses taught at the centre go toward the diploma or certificate in various disciplines that are popular with the job market. The postgraduate courses include the diploma and the master's in business administration.

The choice of the site for the postgraduate courses is ideal. It is strategically located, surrounded by other private providers. This reality is a tangible challenge and since the centre was established it has inspired IAMTECH to prove the reasons for its existence. It means that the institution has to justify its claims as one of the best in the most relevant courses which will equip students with the necessary skills and qualifications. To be honest to the institution's stakeholders, it is gratifying to state that the institution has been proving its mettle. In most of the competitive job areas in the land, IAMTECH is proud to have filled in the vacancies.

# PART ELEVEN

# 38

# Innovation

I have discussed the origins and philosophy behind the establishment of the postgraduate programmes at the Circular Road Learning Centre. It has not been a fruitless endeavour. Besides the gains it has made already, all the indications point to the promising message of a brighter future.

The programmes are well structured and have the blessings of the professional staff at IAMTECH, who have worked assiduously and boosted the profile of the college. The beauty is that whilst the composition of the lecturing staff is very attractive and commands respect they are a blend of domestic and external members. They all have different reasons why they enrolled on the programmes. Some of the domestic lecturers are pursuing various courses at postgraduate diploma level.

Most of the students are mature students. Some are senior managers in business and government enterprises. They have risen through the ranks in their jobs. It is the case that they are all determined to acquire more qualifications adding more leverage to the experiences they have gained already on the job.

For instance, there are senior managers working in the procurement sections of their companies. Others work for the government in other capacities. Senior staffs in the Sierra Leone Army and Police Force have enrolled on the courses. They stand to gain enormously on successful completion of their studies.

I have realized that the moment you talk of postgraduate diploma courses, people's minds run to the teaching profession. Most students pursuing the postgraduate diplomas may not necessarily become professional teachers or lecturers after graduation. Some want to utilize their qualifications to further their education in the same disciplines, related ones or other disciplines.

There are those who are keen on enhancing their prospects for higher promotions in their jobs. Others might utilize their qualifications by seeking out greener pastures. One of the applicants remarked. "There are many chances out there one only needs to acquire the right qualifications. The sky becomes your limit"

Like all the other centres run by IAMTECH, to gain admission at the Circular Road Centre, applicants have to meet the criteria stipulated by the Ministry of Education. They are required to go through continuous assessments and final examinations followed by projects. They are then deemed qualified and are offered the qualifications they deserve.

Establishing the programmes at this and other centres, I have said has some strategic importance. The programmes as well as the centres serve as catalysts for achieving IAMTECH's short and long term goals and strategic advantages. We should remind ourselves that although there are other providers around this same venue at Circular Road, yet students rush to the courses offered by IAMTECH. That indicates that IAMTECH has not only made impressions on the populace but has a competitive advantage over other private providers. It had been proved beyond all doubts that IAMTECH's postgraduate courses are the favourites in town. This means that the institution has earned the respect and dignity it truly deserves as qualified to run postgraduate courses in Sierra Leone.

Who are the appropriate people to comment on the general performances of the programmes? I think the stakeholders deserve the right to comment. I asked some of them to comment on the general performances of the lecturers and management as well as the suitability of the programmes and the management structure.

First, the programme leader at the time commented as follows:

"The courses are viable," said Mr Thomas. Then he thought further and said, "I shall divide my comments into three key areas of performance as follows"

"First is the issue of enrolment, and by that I mean the number of entrants on the courses we offer at the centre. In this area, for just over one year, our data shows that we have done tremendously well. We have met all our targets for all the courses"

"Second is the area of retention. Our records also show that there is a remarkable correlation between our massive enrolments and the number of students we retain and encourage to complete their courses"

"Finally, the quality of our provision and the professionalism of our lecturers, the indicators have ascertained my claim that they have been awesome. The professionalism of the lecturers has yielded immense results since we commenced the courses at this centre"

"My general assessment and verdict is that I can surely state with pride that the centre and its team of lecturers have registered tremendous results of real success. We are very much proud of our efforts, and as for the cooperation of our students, they deserve commendation"

The examinations department of any institution is the lynchpin of that institution. Institutions must do their utmost in order to protect and preserve the quality of assessments. I asked Mr Thomas to comment on the examination procedures they have in place.

"We have robust examinations procedures. Quality is preserved through our disciplined procedures. In that sense we follow and practice strict guidelines at the centre and all IAMTECH learning centres"

The Pro Chancellor is one of the brains behind the inception of the course. She had this to say. "I am gratified that our dream has come true. The overall performances of the postgraduate course underpin one salient point. We deserve autonomous university status. We truly do because we have shown to the authorities, the nation and other private providers that we are up to the tasks and therefore we are qualified to offer postgraduate courses"

The deans and heads of department are going to seize this opportunity and make this innovation count for the benefits of themselves and their students and the country at large. They are not new to the logical analysis that when new courses are introduced in educational institutions, they have to be harnessed meticulously.

That the Learning Centre at Circular Road has started attracting students does not mean that the team should relax and say that they have attained their goals. The centre promises huge success provided considerable capital is invested in the staffing, teaching and learning resources. Logistics and teaching methodology are areas worth reviewing.

The centre hasn't built its own structures for now therefore students make use of the library at the Kissy Dockyards Centre. Innovative lecturers, capable of thinking on their feet, could integrate library studies in their timetable. Give them homework that will get them glued to the library at the institute's headquarters in Kissy Dockyards. New teaching methods will be vital for the success of the centre. The good news is that despite the fact that the centre is housed in rented buildings, when he was leader of the centre, Mr Thomas and his colleagues did the centre and IAMTECH as a whole proud. Students were encouraged to utilize the resources in the library at the main campus, in Kissy Dockyards and they were highly motivated.

By the time this book is completed, Mr Thomas will have assumed the role of an assistant to Dr Fullah, the dean of students and distance learning director of the college.

# 39

# Reflections

Below is a collection of selected speeches made by the senior management team, the crème of IAMTECH. There is also a summary of a paper presented at the celebrations of the nationwide Week of Education. The speeches are found in the college's student handbook and prospectus for 2015. They are presented here in modified version and not in the order in which they were made in the brochures. The reflections of the author recorded here were borne out of the role he played as public orator of the college and were presented in a speech during the 2015 convocation ceremony. It was a special convocation in his view that surpassed other convocations he had attended at IAMTECH.

i. Noble Desk of the CEO

We open this chapter with the welcome address delivered by the co-founding chairperson and chief executive officer Professor Dr Paul Kamara. He is the unassuming personality with the brains of an innovator and visionary. This address clarifies key points which are relevant to students, the administrative staff and members of the public at large.

> I would like to seize this opportunity to welcome our new as well as continuing students to the Institute of Advanced Management and Technology. On behalf of the Principal Dr (Mrs) Lauretta Will-Sillah, members of the Faculty and Staff of IAMTECH, I would like to emphasize that you have made the right choice. It is one that will fetch you enormous opportunities in your life. We are here to mould and imbibe in you the values and determination to serve Country and Humanity.
>
> Over the years, my wife, who is also co-founder of this great institution, Dr Mrs Abie Paula Kamara and I have been in the forefront of its day-to-day management. I would like to inform you formally that we have taken a backseat. We shall operate in our capacity as chairpersons of the IAMTECH Board of Trustees. We

shall still continue to give the maximum support to our new team, led by Dr Mrs Lauretta Will-Sillah and her two Vice Principals and adjutants. Members of this new team are Professor Taylor and Dr Wundah.

We are in the state of transition, meaning that they need our fervent support so that the transition will be smooth and successful. We are quite sure that we shall transit successfully and productively for the good of all of us at IAMTECH. I appeal to you all to work together as a great team in order to realize the full benefits of our dreams.

We are going to prepare your mindset so that you will be placed in good stead in order to contribute productively to the socioeconomic development of this nation. For you the new students in particular, plans have been put in place in order to get your feet on the ground. You have been offered a study guide which will act as your first aid booklet.

It is very essential as it will assist you in the necessary orientations you need in order to approach the academic rigours and challenges and successful completion of your respective courses. In addition, the handbook will provide you with the necessary information you need to know about our rich teaching and learning resources and the other services that the college provides in all its satellite campuses around the country.

Here at IAMTECH, we are always breaking new ground and that has boosted the confidence of our students and the trust society has invested in us. I would admonish you to maximize our enormous opportunities on offer to your full advantage. Despite the ravages of the Ebola epidemic in our country, when it was at its peak, our institution still remained active in terms of teaching and learning.

I am proud to inform you that we were the only institution in the country that literally took learning to our students through our effective hi-tech teaching and learning system. Our massive breathtaking efforts were gracefully recognized during the recent matriculation.

During the matriculation we recorded the highest intakes of new students, over 500 of them enrolled on various courses. Our courses and qualifications are tailored to meet the demands of the competitive job markets within and without Sierra Leone. They also meet the various needs of our students.

During our recent convocation ceremony we awarded degrees, diplomas and certificates to over 500 students that successfully completed their programmes. The awards illustrate and underpin the fact that we are an institution that has made a mark in the tertiary sector as well as the job market. We are also a tertiary institution to reckon with within and without this country.

Our success stories are due to the degree of discipline we espouse and practice at the highest level. IAMTECH like all quality educational institutions around the world operates on the basis of a social contract signed between the institution and its students.

We provide valuable lessons, skills and qualification for our students and guide them in the routines that will prepare them for life's challenges and promises. We instruct and mould our students in such a manner that they become self-sufficient and capable of contributing their own quota to national development as good and functionally productive citizens.

In honouring the social contract that binds you and this great institution, you on the other hand are expected to take your studies seriously and obey the rules and regulations of this institution. Hence it is important for both parties that is IAMTECH and you, the students, as signatories of the social contract to abide by the provisions that bind your relationship.

The rationales for the founding of this college you have rightly chosen to attend are beneficial for all and sundry. They are rooted in the need to alleviate the endemic poverty as well as the related social vices that have affected the socioeconomic development of our country, Sierra Leone. These endemic vices have been well documented by numerous local and international experts, including commentators, and theorists as part and parcel of the causal analysis of the debilitating civil war.

We have a duty to accomplish. We have to work tirelessly and alleviate the causes of our national problems. We can only be well placed if we live and perform according to the values of our motto. It is "For Country and For Humanity" It inspired us as the proprietors and founders of this institution of which we are all invaluable stakeholders. We have to work hard in order to inspire others to help reduce poverty and illiteracy and create a better country for the benefit of all and sundry.

We offer wide ranging courses and we are proud of our great team of professionally trained and well qualified, experienced academicians employed to lecture and advise you about the great values of life. They will instruct you in your interpersonal skills and help you learn to respect the laws of your communities and society at large.

Our courses on offer include accounting and finance, logistics and procurement, management, business, banking, development economics, Information Computer Technology, professional short courses, Communication skills, and foundation in English Language and academic writing schemes.

In addition to the main campus at the Kissy Dockyards, IAMTECH is spread across the length and breadth of the country. It has campuses or learning centres at the Circular Road and Young Women's Christian Association (YWCA), Rokupr, Kambia, Lunsar, Bo and Kono. Plans are in the pipeline to establish learning centres in Lungi and Makeni. Like the main campus, these satellite learning centres offer quality courses and teaching and learning facilities.

We pride ourselves on quality assurance and audit as it is the backbone of any viable educational institution. Therefore, quality is the cornerstone of our trademarks. We have been recognized as the best tertiary college in the country by our peers, the media and the public at large. This recognition is due to the quality learning we provide backed by proactive disciplinary measures in order to ensure that quality assurance and audit are maintained at all times.

We are a liberal institution and therefore we stand by those values that facilitate learning as a public good. Our programmes, facilities and opportunities are not limited to a handpicked few. We serve everyone and everywhere, hence our outreach strategies of providing learning are spread across the length and breadth of Sierra Leone.

We believe that when educational opportunities and rights are spread widely for the common good, it will guarantee a legacy for future generations of good, responsible and successful citizens and leaders. That is the ideal type of education mankind seeks.

I would like to conclude by way of admonition. Don't forget that education and the pursuit of knowledge does not end at the doorsteps of educational institutions. The purpose of education is not limited to the acquisition of paper qualifications and securing of lucrative jobs.

Therefore, at the completion of your valuable courses, don't forget to: "Go to the people. Live with them. Learn from them. Love them. Start with what they know. Build with what they have. Don't forget that like the best leaders, when the work is done, the task accomplished, then the people will say with the wisdom of the Great Chinese philosopher, Lao Tzu (700 BC): We have done this ourselves.

## ii. Noble Desk of the Principal (Dr Mrs Luaretta Will-Sillah)

"Give a man a fish and he eats a day, teach the man to fish and he eats a life-time"

On behalf of the institute's faculty and staff, I welcome you all to this great institution of higher learning. As your new principal, it is my duty to open all avenues to you during your time in this college, so that together, we can fulfil the mission and vision of IAMTECH. Our mission and vision here at IAMTECH is to enable you to meaningfully experience the essential purpose of tertiary education and enjoy the inherent benefits you will derive out of it.

There is an adage that teaches a significant wisdom. It says thus: "Give a man a fish and he eats a day, teach the man to fish and he eats a life-time" The wisdom found in this adage is the driving force, the vehicle of the aims and objectives of this great college of ours.

It simply means that we are here to prepare our students so well that they will be able to serve themselves, their country and humanity. It simply means that we should equip our students with the relevant skills and qualifications and values that will make them independent. We should prepare them adequately enough to break the yoke, the chain of dependency and make them self-reliant.

They need to be self-reliant so that they are not rendered so handicapped to the extent they forever rely on the government for their day-to-day survival. In short, IAMTECH is here to ensure the dependency culture is eliminated in our individual homes, communities and country at large.

I want to state on behalf of my colleagues that as a seasoned, tertiary institution, IAMTECH will nurse and nurture a lofty idealism around the values of our aims and objectives like all viable institutions ought to do. This institution is no stranger to those stipulated values. They espouse an unwavering commitment to service to country and humanity.

We shall achieve these goals by equipping the best and brightest and enabling the ones that need help in order to attain the maximum level of their potentials. The brightest among you, this institution shall mould their mindsets and talents in order to attain excellence in their studies and other related endeavours. Our programmes and methods of delivery are not a one sided pedagogy.

We deliver lessons through face-to-face and Open and Distance Learning methods. Through the combinations of these two effective methods, we have been able to take learning to the unreachable in our communities around the country, especially in the rural areas. Our programmes and the periods we run our classes are flexible.

We take into consideration the needs of mature, adult learners and those that are in employment. Thus, we run effective shifts programmes morning and evening sessions. Some classes are conducted on Saturdays, all aimed at suiting the needs and personal circumstances of students.

In this part of the world, open and distance learning are new. I am proud to say that with IAMTECH, our capable lecturers have firm grips on how to deliver them to good effect. We have already made a huge impact on the minds of our numerous, open and distance students out there. They know the value of the model of learning that is why they keep enrolling on the programmes. IAMTECH has an impressive track record because of its multidimensional methods of teaching.

Sitting side-by-side with the proactive promotion of Distance and Open Learning is our corporate professional schemes. We offer these courses through our open and distance learning methods with the efficient use of information and computer technology. Our track records show that once our students complete these courses, they will kill two birds with one stone. They will not only earn well-paid jobs, they will become stakeholders in the socioeconomic development of the nation.

We have come a long way and along this route, there is no turning back. The maximization of success is our ultimate goal. That goal is to gain accredited, autonomous university status. We face a period of transition in the history of this institution. Hence it is gratifying that having served our pupilage successfully under Njala University, for the past four years, we are mature to attain autonomous university status.

I am glad to inform you that we have put in our application formally for university autonomy, which is undergoing the necessary processes at the Tertiary Education Commission. It requires all hands on deck in order to attain this landmark achievement in the history of IAMTECH. The twenty-fourth year of the founding of IAMTECH is drawing closer. It is a significant milestone for us all in the IAMTECH family. We are going to make sure that the celebrations are marked by the pomp and pageant it truly deserves.

On behalf of my entire staff, I want to assure you that we will put our shoulders to the wheel and attain our goals together for the benefit of us all. We are here to inject new ideas and improve on those ideas that were initiated by those before us. We live in changing and challenging times. We need to embrace ourselves the challenges that are posed by the changing times and maximize the opportunities they offer.

Once more, I want to reiterate that we shall do our utmost with the backing of the founders and financiers, governing council and the rest of the workforce in order to make this great and productive college of ours one of the best institutions in post war Sierra Leone.

### iii. Noble Desk of the Vice Principal Academic Affairs

This is a summary of the paper presented at a symposium at the Miata Conference Center by Professor Patrick FU Taylor of IAMTECH. It is here reproduced as summarized by the rapporteur of the symposium. It was mentioned alongside other presentations in the country's leading newspapers during the nationwide celebrations of the Week of Education 7 to 12 December 2015. The events were officially launched by HE President Dr Ernest Bai Koroma and Dr Minkailu Bah, Minister of Education Science and Technology.

The title of the paper is "Quality Education for Sustainable Development in the 21$^{st}$ Century".

> Professor Taylor observed that Education for Sustainable Development (ESD) emerged out of the Sustainable Development agenda initiated by the UN General Assembly in 1987. Subsequently, he said, the UN General Assembly in its fifty-seventh resolution declared 2005 to 2014 as ESD decade with UNESCO in the driving seat. He pointed out that the ongoing UN Paris Conference (30 November to 11 December) made a binding agreement of over 130 countries on ESD.

> Professor Taylor observed that there are competing definitions of 'Sustainability' and re-echoed the UN 1987

definition of 'sustainable development' as "the development that meets the needs of the present without jeopardizing future generations to meet their own needs". He suggested that ESD is an important educational tool which is about awareness raising and knowledge promotion for people from all walks of life (from the driver to the farmer, from the manufacturer to the petty trader) as to how to make the world "more livable for ours and future generations".

Thus according to the UK-sponsored guide (2014) on ESD, Education for Sustainable Development is "the process of equipping students with the knowledge and understanding, skills and attributes needed to work and live in a way that safeguards environmental, social and economic wellbeing, both in the present and for the future"

Professor Taylor explained how ESD feeds into the Sustainable Development (Education) Goal: ESD Learning Performance Framework provides a basis for setting up measurable qualitative targets leading to "universal quality education that provides the necessary life-skills for individual wellbeing while also empowering society with the capacity for realizing sustainable future for all", in short, Education for Sustainable Development plus Quality Education equals Quality Education for Sustainable Development. He suggested that three interconnected sets of environment, social and economic factors underpin SD (and by implication ESD) He went on to outline the UN's five strategic objectives for SD in Sub-Saharan Africa as follows:

1. Improving political harmonization and commitment for the implementation of ESD at country and regional levels.

2. Broadening public awareness on and strengthening the principles and practice of sustainable development in individual and collective lives.

3. Promoting education that is supported by African culture and contributes to sustainable social and economic development.

4. Improving the quality of education for sustainable development.

5. Consolidating and diversifying partnerships around ESD.

Professor Taylor went on to suggest that ESD concerns, and must involve, the whole community, it is a multidisciplinary concept and an inter-ministerial initiative, which must be embedded into people's lifestyle by the use of all known methods, and it calls for urgent and critical action to ensure human survival. He concluded that ESD issues, challenges and mitigating measures are bound to vary from community to community and for different sectors.

Reactions:

A member of the audience asked the following question: "We are not serious about maintaining a healthy environment and taking these into consideration how do we ensure sustainable development?" In his response Professor Taylor suggested, 'There has to be legislative backing to all our efforts. The Environmental Protection Agency is the only institution advocating for environmental protection and we need a concerted effort, and to legislate and make it a national issue.'

iv. Noble Desk of Vice Principal Administration and Public Orator

I have many sweet and meaningful memories of IAMTECH, which can fill a whole book. For the sake of brevity, I'll rather keep it crispy but informative. By the end of the year 2014, one of the worst years in the history of Sierra Leone misfortunes, Professor Kamara rang me in London one evening. I thought it was the usual calls he makes when there is some urgent matter to deal with. I must confess that I have been their distance handyman, a role we have both managed very well with remarkable success.

'My brother,' he commenced, 'We thank God the Ebola epidemic is close to over now. We need to ensure that these students graduate in the early or mid month of 2015.'

The moment he mentioned the word graduation, I knew that he was going to remind me about my usual role, that of the institute's public orator. I listened with keen ears and decided to seek the opinion and consent of my wife. She is a keen supporter of the Kamara family and is amazed at the progress their project has made. Without much deliberation over the matter, she gave me her undivided consent. 'You are allowed to go it is a worthy course,' she said with a beautiful smile.

The role of public orator at convocation ceremonies is a vital one. The public orator is meant to add spice to the speeches and create spectacular angles to the commentaries and entire ceremony. Since it is a ceremony full of pomp and pageants, the public orator should sharpen his or her power of oratory and rhetoric and combine both tactfully. The orator should bring the written words alive, through the sweet and golden tongue. Surely, it should be similar to that of the Queen of Sheba. It should be a sugar-coated tongue.

One analyst put it quite forcefully.

"A public orator should have the power to mesmerize and move the audience to the state of pathos. At their best, powerful speakers who perform the role of public orators at convocation ceremonies have the ability to reduce their audiences to tears. They could be tears of joy or sadness either way, the bottom line is that public orators are gifted with the powers to mesmerize people."

I must reveal that I have done countless public speaking appearances some of which I can hardly recall. It has been a long time since I appeared on stage during which I performed various roles. They range from reviewing books on stage to junior and senior convocation ceremonies at various places in different countries. This is not about any form of self glorification, but upon reflection, I think I have done well.

With regards to my role as public orator at IAMTECH's convocation ceremonies, I have performed as public orator on three occasions. The first was in 2011, during which my role called for a passive performance. It was during the Chancellorship of Professor Abu Sesay who was replaced towards the end of 2015 by Professor Ernest Ndomahina.

I was not given the room to display my power of oratory and rhetoric. By virtue of the affiliation understanding between Njala University and IAMTECH, the former calls the shots for the latter's convocation. They give the approval but by mutual consents, they set the date of the ceremony.

Most importantly, Njala University confers the degree, diploma, higher diplomas and certificates on the occasion. Hence, the ceremonies are performed under the auspices of Njala University, but on the campus of IAMTECH. Technically, Njala University may have the seal of approval and conferment of the various qualifications but IAMTECH hosts them hence the ceremony is conducted on its premises.

In 2015, I attended the third convocation ceremony.

It was after I assumed the role of Vice Principal Administration of the college. I arrived in Freetown in March and the ceremony was held on Saturday, 23 May. Like the previous ones, it was spectacular, and I equally rose to the occasion. The reason this particular one was special was that it coincided with the college's bidding to gain autonomous university status.

The power to grant university status to tertiary colleges rests with the Tertiary Education Commission (TEC). I have to reiterate that this institution is one of the most powerful ambits of the educational system in Sierra Leone because without its seal of approval, no tertiary institution has the right to operate as a university in the country. As the public orator of the institution, it was my singular honour to popularize and publicize our bid.

I was very much conscious of the demands of this singular honour given to me on that occasion, so I used the power of oratory but more of rhetoric to advertise and sell the idea, ideals, rationale and the massive benefits IAMTECH will gain if it is granted an accredited, autonomous university status in the near future. In the previous preceding chapters I have discussed at length the inherent politics and broader benefits of the autonomous university status that IAMTECH seeks. There is no room for me to rehearse them in this chapter, so I need to move on.

Generally, it was actually in the final two convocations which were held in 2013 and 2015 that I was given the room to do justice to my gorgeous title "Public Orator"

It is sad to reflect that in 2014 almost all facets of the country were put out of business. The country was forced to temporarily suspend all classes and other activities in the education sector due to the Ebola epidemic.

Therefore, there were no convocations activities because all educational institutions were shut down, except in the latter part of 2015. During that period thankfully, there were signs that the ravages of the epidemic were receding.

As luck would have it the very movers and shakers of matters at the TEC and Ministry of Education Science and Technology were present at the convocation ceremony of 2015. They were there in their official capacity. The Executive Secretary of the TEC, a senior representative of the ministry and the Pro Chancellor of Fourah Bay College graced the occasion.

We even had a special guest of honour the wife of the Minister of Education Science and Technology, Dr Minkailu Bah. I recognized the importance of the presence of all these dignitaries. I sprang into full swing and released my tongue to good effect, wooing each and every one of them to recognize the inherent logic behind IAMTECH's application for accredited autonomous university status.

Ambitions like the dream to succeed are boundless in humanity. Especially, people become proactively restless and pursue their goals through tireless hope. IAMTECH has the ambitions to dream and dream big in chasing all the good things that will bring prosperity to this nation, including autonomous university status. Prior to the ceremony on that Saturday, it had been debated in senior management circles as to whether we should hang a banner with the inscription *University of Management and Technology (UNIMTECH)* or simply stick to our current name IAMTECH.

*Dr. Michael Nicolas Wundah*

Obviously, it was unanimously agreed that we should dream big, so we went for the name with the university. It instinctively justifies and crowns the big dreams the college has at heart. It was a big statement of intent and determination to acquire university status in the land, so there was no better platform to make that known apart from the one that was created on that day.

As a mark of homage and glorious tribute to the sacrifices of the founding figures, the husband and wife Paul and Paula, we named the amphitheatre after the first name of the wife. It was named the Abie Amphitheatre. The colourful stage was set and the engine to synchronize the sweet melodies of combined, gallant ambitions and statements of determination were left to the public orator to articulate and articulate well I did.

This project is the baby of both husband and wife, so it was fitting to officially recognize the tireless contributions of the two personalities on that historic day before that august body. We had planned to carve a handsome image of the man himself, who refers to himself as "Paul Getty". Things didn't go as planned initially.

However, as the saying goes, there should always be an alternative plan in case things go wrong. We improvised a plan B in less than forty-eight hours to the D-Day which we executed to maximum effect. A sweet note of appreciation was written and read as a citation to the convocation gathering on that day.

Our eminent personality and recipient was not informed about the award it was meant to be a sweet and memorable surprise. Paul Kamara is a shy and an unassuming personality. The moment his name was announced and he was ushered to the podium, beads of tears ran down his two cheeks. It took us almost half an hour to console this unassuming soul of harmless man. He listened to the citation carefully, and then gracefully received a small certificate of appreciation.

It was fitted into a nice photo glasslike album. I couldn't hold back my own tears, so together we shed them all the same as tears of joy and sweet memories. The rationale behind the award or prize was a reminder that the efforts of people, no matter how little they are, must be recognized. Gratitude, they say, is one of the articles of faith.

# Notes of Selected Sources

1. Week in Education 2015, MEST Documents

2. Education Act 2004, MEST

3. Concept Document of IAMTECH 2010

4. 6334 Education Dispensation, 1992, MEST Documents

5. Interviews at various times with Professor Paul Kamara and Dr Mrs Abie Paula Kamara

6. Interviews at various times with the deans, heads of departments of IAMTECH

7. Interviews at various times with the Examinations Department IAMTECH

8. Interviews at various times with heads of other learning centres of IAMTECH

9. Interviews with at various times with heads of other learning centres

10. Week in Education 2015 Minis try of Education Science and Technology (MEST), Sierra Leone

11. Symposium and Seminars Week in Education 2015 Miata Conference Centre 7- 12 December 2015

12. IAMTECH brochure/prospectus for 2012

13. IAMTECH brochure/ prospectus for 2013

14. IAMTECH brochures/ prospectus for 2014

15. IAMTECH brochure/prospectus 2015/2016

16. Report Published by the Working Group on Distance Learning and Open Learning in Sub-Sahara Africa, 2012

17. Samples of selected unpublished dissertations (10) all case studies relating to IAMTECH, submitted by students of IAMTECH-diplomas an Degree course 2010-2014

18. Samples of selected unpublished dissertations (10) all case studies related to IAMTECH, submitted by students of IAMTECH covering diplomas and degrees 2014 and 2015.

# Bibliography

1.  Giddens A, 2004, The Third Way and its Critics, Polity Press

2.  Olowu D, Williams A, Soremekun K, 1999, CODESRIA, Dakar, Senegal

3.  Rose JD 1970, Introduction TO Sociology, Fredonia NY

4.  Stephenson J and Yorke Mantz, 1998, Capability and Quality in Higher Education, Kogan Page Limited, London

5.  Wundah M.N 2004, Sunset In Sierra Leone, The Book Guild Ltd, East Sussex, England

6.  Wundah MN, 2014, Reach IN for the Stars, Biography of Dr Christiana Ayeka Thorpe, Author House, UK

7.  Wundah M.N, 1995, 'Analytical Study of the 6334 Education Reform in Sierra Leone, Institute of Education London University

Printed in the United States
By Bookmasters